All the Queens Houses

jovis

All the Queens Houses

An Architectural Portrait
of New York's Largest and
Most Diverse Borough

Rafael Herrin-Ferri

Foreword

Rafael Herrin-Ferri

Twelve years ago my wife and I decided to move out of Manhattan in pursuit of more space, cheaper rent, and a much needed break from the bustling metropolis. We wound up in Sunnyside, a neighborhood in the northwestern section of Queens developed as a bedroom community in the 1920s and 1930s. It consists mainly of six-story, brick apartment buildings straddling a large boulevard (Queens Boulevard) with an elevated subway running down the middle.

Manhattan still felt very close: physically and in spirit. Fifteen minutes on the 7-train gets you into Grand Central Station, and a twenty minute bus ride to the southeast corner of Central Park. You can even bike over the Queensboro bridge in about the same time if you prefer. New York's two most iconic buildings—the Empire State Building and the Chrysler Building—stand like beacons at the end of most streets when you look west. Even though our home address was now in a different borough, it didn't quite seem as if we had left "the City." Not for the first few months, at least.

As we started to venture further away from the boulevard and the zone of brick apartment buildings, we soon discovered the low-rise housing styles Queens is typically associated with. Then we understood why some New Yorkers—often pejoratively—refer to it as an "outer borough." At times, it does feel as if you are in the suburbs.

In the northern section of Sunnyside is the historic district of Sunnyside Gardens, inspired by the English Garden City movement. It is composed of modest two-story brick row houses that are deferential to the green spaces of the master plan (front gardens, communal gardens, pedestrian footpaths, mews). Most have vestibule extensions at the front and a few have added third floors or dormers that face the rear. All of these informal alterations came to an end (contentiously) in 2007 when the district was officially given its landmark status in an attempt to keep the original architecture tasteful and property values high.

To the south of Queens Boulevard, a couple of avenues in, are similar size houses, also in a traditional style but without the landmark designation. These have clashing alterations (visible from all angles), a mix of different roof profiles, larger window sizes, and more accent colors. In most cases, they have traded their front yards for a patio or parking space. Kitschy precast ornaments abound. This section of the neighborhood also feels suburban but much less so than its counterpart to the north.

As I explored it further, one particular house stopped me dead in my tracks. It was perched on top of a deli at a forty-five degree angle producing two triangular terraces and a third off of the top floor, each with its respective polycarbonate awnings. Granted, this *Sun Deli Penthouse* (p. 47), as I have titled it in the book, was significantly more idiosyncratic than most of the other houses I had seen in our neighborhood up until that point, but it did seem to showcase a very different attitude towards residential architecture in this new borough I was now calling "home." I had to explore it some more.

With my compact wide-angle camera and iPhone I began to wander into the nearby neighborhoods in search of more "Queens vernacular." First I explored Woodside, then Astoria; after that, Ditmars-Steinway, and then Long Island City. Each was filled with everyday "gems"—some at "Sun Deli" levels of exhibitionism and others with more subtle, "accidental" beauty, resulting from years of incremental alterations. The examples seemed never ending.

At the beginning of my impromptu photo-survey project, I would just let the houses guide me from one gem to the next. You could see them waiting for you at the end of the street or the next block over. Houses filled with personality, ready to seize the attention of all who passed by.

A freewheeling quality defined the first six months of the project, which was well suited to the subject matter, my main modes of transportation (bicycle and skateboard), and the leisure time I had set aside for it. But the more houses I would find, the more seemed to be out there, and the more I feared I would miss the best ones. This new collector's style of thinking led me to swap my casual meanderings for a more systematic, block-by-block approach that would eventually lead me to a full-blown, borough-wide survey. When the title for the project, "All the Queens Houses," popped into my head that sealed the deal. My father, a novelist and literature professor, joked I had made a "Faustian bargain." He was not altogether wrong.

As my surveying methods got more methodical, I also began to standardize the photography format: a horizontal house-portrait style from the opposite side of the street, which included neighbors. Street trees, and parked cars, seemed to capture the architectural character and context best. Naturally, there were houses that warranted a good close-up that would require the image to be rotated, but for the most part the aim was to produce a series of residential structures that could easily be compared and contrasted when placed side by side, in a more "scientific" manner. For this, consistent lighting conditions were key.

After experimenting with shoots on sunny days, I opted to follow in the footsteps of Bernd and Hilla Becher with a good dose of cloud cover. Varying amounts of direct sunlight were distorting the true colors of the structures and casting long shadows that would obscure the most interesting features. This made the act of surveying easier since both sides of the street were cast in the same light, allowing me to complete discrete sections of a neighborhood at the same time. I also believe it enhanced my peripheral vision, allowing me to spot details more easily since all was bathed in the same diffuse lighting. The downside was being on constant "cloud patrol," i.e., tracking the weather on three different apps to see if I was going to go survey the next morning before work or have a full day on the weekend to take the train out to one of the more far-flung neighborhoods in the borough.

On one of these "fine" cloudy days in February of 2020—approximately seven years after I had taken my first photographs of Queens houses—I was able to complete the survey. Quite fittingly, it was in the neighborhood of Far Rockaway. It was "far out" indeed, both in terms of distance—almost two hours of travel time from my apartment door in Woodside—and in the mix of housing styles. Including its subsections of Bayswater and Wave Crest, these Far Rockaway streets contained a grab bag of Queens typologies mixed in with some unique local ones: the beach bungalows. I was glad I saw it last.

On the train ride back, I reflected on the vast sea of low-rise housing I had spent the last seven years surveying as much of it went by my window. Truth be told, from the twenty-foot elevation of the tracks it all pretty much looks the same. (From the window seat of the airplanes landing at the two local airports, this is even more the case.) The wide variety of character traits that I have tried to capture in the following photographs is really only perceptible from street level. Perhaps this is the quality of the Queens vernacular that I have found so refreshing, that it is human scaled and can only really be appreciated from a human perspective on the ground.

Thinking back to my years in Manhattan, I recall there was also a lot of character at street level, but almost all of it was related to retail and restaurants (besides the people, of course). It existed mainly for consumption. In contrast, the character of Queens is almost entirely defined by the personal and cultural preferences of its small-scale property owners. It is for the most part a corporate-free zone defined by clusters of similarly minded peoples providing for one another. The village character of its original townships persists—the houses have just changed hands and it has all become more of a "global village" in the last several decades—the most diverse community in America, as Joseph Heathcott points out in his introductory essay.

In many ways, the "World's Borough"—as it is known locally—seems like an everyday reincarnation of the two World's Fairs that Queens hosted in 1939–40 and 1964–65 at Flushing Meadows-Corona Park. There is a festive, international quality about its streetscape—albeit a little scrappy at times—that borrows heavily from the various traditions around the globe. Many of the international cuisines that can be sampled on the streets of what is now the food mecca of New York were first introduced to Americans at these fairs. But it is equally rich in culture and spirituality as evidenced by the many smaller museums and houses of worship that are sprinkled throughout the borough. Again, both of these elements were represented at the fairs, especially the 1964–65 one, with several religious pavilions mixed into the International Area, the most prominent being the Vatican, with Michelangelo's *Pietà* on display.

Architecturally, Queens houses (and multi-family structures) can also remind one of the attention-grabbing designs of expo pavilions, not only because of their often cartoonish interpretations of traditional styles (see *Astoria Citadel*, *Minoan Makeover*, and *Queen Anne Cartoon*) but also due to their elaborate "front-of-house" features including dynamic paving patterns, ramps, stairs, etc. (see *Copacabana, Queens*, *Raised Ranch in Wonderland*, and *Gate House*). But the majority are more modest affairs which have simply applied extraneous materials, paint colors, and ornaments in whatever quantities they can afford at any given time.

One Colombian woman I spoke with explained how she installed a brow of Spanish tile over the garage door of her gray stone Tudor to make it feel a little more like home. A Guyanese man also shared with me his rationale for painting his entire Queen Anne Victorian turquoise: to remind him of the Caribbean Sea. If you walk around southwestern Queens you might be surprised to find dozens of precast concrete elephants capping brick fence posts. These are meant to recreate, on a very vernacular level, the "elephant gates" common throughout the Indian subcontinent.

For me, the cultural dimension of conducting this survey was just as enjoyable as the act of discovering and "collecting" idiosyncratic houses. It served as a vehicle to "see the world"—at least the cheek by jowl condensed version of it that exists in Queens, New York. The format I adopted for the book, broken down by "geographic" sections and neighborhoods, is meant to evoke the experience of a travel guide. The selection of house portraits is just a small sample of what the "World's Borough" has to offer but one that reflects its incredible diversity. And even though there are no people visible in them, I trust that it is mainly the human spirit that shows through in the architecture.

Woodside, New York
March 2021

Queens is the Future

Joseph Heathcott

If you walk along Northern Boulevard, you will pass a handball court at 80th Street with a mural that announces "Queens is the Future." And well it might be. More than any other place, Queens is a testament to how an increasingly diverse population can fit itself into an already built environment, creatively articulating the urban landscape to suit new needs and purposes. It is a landscape whose very ordinariness and lack of pretension have left it remarkably open to wave after wave of newcomers. It is this ordinary yet open habitat that Rafael Herrin-Ferri explores with such visual eloquence in the pages that follow.

For many New Yorkers, Queens is a "there" without a "there," a cipher, a massive jigsaw puzzle: sprawling, expansive, tangled, multiform, low-slung, and centerless. It offers little of the grandeur and intensity of Manhattan, the dignity and aged charm of Brooklyn, the separatist fervor of Staten Island, or the edginess and renown of The Bronx. It is not "beautiful" in the way that conjures images of Central Park, the Grand Concourse, or Brownstone Brooklyn. There is no Guggenheim or Radio City Music Hall or Lincoln Center. Nobody wrote their *Rockaway Beach Memoirs*, tried to sell the 59th Street Bridge, or declared that "Ladies and Gentlemen, Queens is Burning." It is, quite simply, New York City's most enigmatic borough. And I love it with all of my heart.

In one sense, Queens may seem a study in superlatives. Spreading across 117 square miles, it is the largest borough of the city, constituting fully one-third of the total landmass of New York. With 2.25 million people it is the second most populous borough after Brooklyn, and as a stand alone city would rank fifth in the nation. As a county of the State of New York, it is the most ethnically diverse in the United States; nearly half of all residents are foreign born, and over 85% speak a language other than English in the home. Not surprisingly, it has the largest, busiest, and most multilingual public library system in the United States. And Queens is one of only a handful of the 3000-odd counties in the U.S. where the median income of Black families is higher than that of whites. Often disparaged as the "airport borough," Queens is where the Port Authority operates two of the country's busiest airports, one on the Long Island Sound (LaGuardia) and the other on the Atlantic Ocean (JFK). Queensbridge Houses, the nation's largest public housing project, is located near the East River in Long Island City. Along with Chicago, it is the only place in the U.S. to have hosted two World's Fairs.

But these varied superlatives reveal very little about Queens as a place. Despite its sheer size and diversity, Queens is probably the least coherent of the boroughs. It offers an urbanity distinct from its sister boroughs, but you would be at a loss to describe it. Stretched by the gravitational forces of high-rise Manhattan to the west and low-slung Long Island to the east, it never resolves itself into a discernable whole. An administrative subset of New York City, it presents no center of its own, and endures a historically weak identity as a unit. Unlike Manhattan and Staten Island, Queens is not a self-contained geologic entity; it is one of the four arbitrarily drawn political boundaries that segment Long Island, along with Suffolk, Nassau, and Kings (Brooklyn) counties. While Manhattan marched effortlessly northward through The Bronx, the connection between "The City" and Queens was never a foregone conclusion. And unlike Brooklyn, Queens was never a city in its own right, but rather a county composed of a patchwork of small towns, marshes, trade roads, and farms.

As a result of this multi-nuclear growth, residents today tend to identify intensely with their neighborhoods. Such loyalties are reflected in customary geocoding. Queens residents had been hyphenating their addresses since the advent of regular postal service in the early nineteenth century. In 1911, the city imposed a grid system onto the roiling and confusing landscape of Queens, which erased the dozen Main Streets and Washington Avenues in favor of numbered thoroughfares. This eventually led to 271 numbered north-south streets, places, and lanes, and 161 numbered east-west avenues, roads, drives, and terraces. Soon after, the U.S. Post office proposed to eliminate the hyphenated street numbers and enforce the borough name for the address, but Queens residents resisted these further impositions. Today, for residents of any neighborhood in Brooklyn, the address convention is Brooklyn, NY, while for residents of Flushing in Queens, to take one example, the address convention is Flushing, NY. The U.S. Postal Service has tried many times to squelch these obscure practices, but they endure thanks to the stubbornness of residents and their fierce attachment to local communities.

Meanwhile, the immense volume of ink spilled on the history, culture, and politics of New York City is primarily devoted to events that unfold in Manhattan and, increasingly, Brooklyn. The Bronx erupted into American consciousness during the urban crisis of the 1970s and 1980s as an exemplar of physical decay. The perennial agitation of Staten Island residents for secession from New York City has been grounded in a strong place identity and affinity with New Jersey. But Queens has lurked on the sidelines, despite the fact that it has rapidly become the most diverse place in the nation. Somehow the borough's beaches, trains, airports, expressways, bridges, neighborhoods, shopping malls, and homes have not historically added up to a coherent sense of "Queens" as a place, and today it remains little understood. (For those of us who live here, that is not necessarily a bad thing.)

Nevertheless, at a close grain Queens is a study in variety, as Rafael Herrin-Ferri details so marvelously in this book. Not only is the borough socially diverse; Herrin-Ferri's exhaustive survey reveals that it also contains a tremendous range of housing types, architectural styles, block and street morphologies, and neighborhood forms. So much variety, in fact, that it defies ready categorization or explanation. Thus, in the following pages, I will not try to "explain" Queens—a futile effort that this roiling, changeable, centerless borough will always resist. Rather, I will turn it over, look at its various facets, and perhaps bring some shape and dimension to the borough as a way to contextualize Herrin-Ferri's project.

The Making of a Borough

For much of its history up to the nineteenth century, Queens was home primarily to Dutch and English colonists, a dwindling and dislocated population of Native people, and residents of African descent, including enslaved, manumitted, and freeborn. After the British took control of New Netherland in 1664, they imposed the county system, and established Kings and Queens counties through royal decree in 1683. Renowned for its tolerance of multiple religious and cultural groups, Queens attracted Quakers, Catholics, and eventually Eastern Orthodox and Jewish settlers. Free African men and women established congregations that would endure in various forms across the centuries. Still, the borough grew slowly, with settlement radiating outward from five principal towns of Flushing, Hempstead, Jamaica, Newtown, and Oyster Bay.

Settler colonists brought with them to Queens their varied architectural "pattern languages," mental maps of what a home should look like. Farmers might have initially built distinctly "Dutch" or "English" houses, but over the course of the eighteenth century, they borrowed ideas, technical know-how, and architectural fashions from one another. They also responded to successive waves of style and construction from abroad, mixing framing, roof shape, window forms, and other elements. By the late eighteenth and early nineteenth centuries, the long-established farm families had begun parceling their lands and selling them off into smaller and smaller farmsteads and subdivisions for newcomers, especially around the five towns, principal road junctions, and new train stations. As a result, older rural influences waned over the nineteenth century, as the Dutch and English settler culture of Long Island gave way to second and third generation German and Irish families, New England migrants, and a trickle of upstart transplants from Manhattan.

Still, by the end of the nineteenth century, as Queens merged with four other counties into the Greater City of New York, the borough remained largely a rural landscape of farms and villages. Indeed, the population had grown slowly, from 45,000 after the Civil War to 150,000 in 1900; Kings County, by comparison, had reached over one million residents by the turn of the century. The five principal towns had become bustling, active nodes of marketing and trade, but remained quite small. Newtown village, for example, was still a cluster of thirty to forty households in 1873, with a few gravel streets, a Long Island Railroad station, and a post office. That same year, Flushing, the largest of the towns, boasted some 400 platted properties, though only half of these contained buildings; many remained farmland, marsh, or open fields. Still, an ever-growing network of roads connected residents into an intricate mosaic of villages, farms, and stations that would form the underlying blueprint for the borough's later growth.

Noise of the Hammer, Music of the Saw

The Queens that you will encounter in this book took shape amid the rapid expansion of the city in the twentieth century. This produced a series of competing grids radiating out from old town centers. Where these grids collided, they resolved into obliquely angled streets and sidewalks, oddly shaped parcel geographies, tangled webs of urban fabric. Moreover, the existence of relatively cheap and abundant land for building, the successive waves of architectural revival styles, and a series of accelerated boom and bust cycles have endowed Queens with a highly mixed and haphazard appearance. In this way, the jumbled, multi-form, centerless sprawl of Queens unfolded through the twentieth century as an urban landscape distinct in many ways from that of the other boroughs of New York City.

Over the first three decades of the twentieth century, the population of Queens swelled from 150,000 in 1900 to one million in 1930, with the highest growth rate (130%) in the boom years of the roaring twenties. Most new residents came from the crowded precincts of Manhattan, eager for the light, air, and space promised by real estate promoters. To accommodate this rapid growth, newly platted residential grids appeared almost overnight. "Where potatoes were hoed until a year or two ago," the Queens Chamber of Commerce effused in their 1920 report, "are now located streets of attractive homes. On every block throughout the Borough the noise of the hammer and the music of the saw is heard, and yet, with all this building activity, the demand for homes is unprecedented."

These new bits of nascent urban fabric grew in fits and starts from the five principal towns, or found purchase on isolated rural farmsteads and marshlands. Sometimes developers would sell off parcels and homebuilding would commence even before streets were laid; other times paved streets and sewers awaited property buyers. In the first decade of the twentieth century, the most rapid growth occurred in Western Queens, particularly Long Island City and Astoria. Over the next two decades, this growth shifted to the vast tracts of land in the "Second Ward," including neighborhoods like Elmhurst, Corona, Forest Hills, Maspeth, Middle Village, Woodside, and Glendale. However uneven in space and time, all of this investment of labor, capital, and energy created a patchwork mosaic of subdivisions and settlements that grew together and filled in over time. It is this crazy quilt quality that most distinguishes the urban landscape and built environment of Queens.

This rapid expansion was made possible by a succession of large-scale infrastructure projects that tightened the connection of Queens to Manhattan. The completion of the 59th Street Bridge set the stage for the borough's inexorable growth, replacing the sluggish ferries and allowing for automobile and trolley traffic. The trolley system itself, already threaded through several neighborhoods, expanded to nearly all parts of the borough by the 1920s. Following closely on the heels of the new bridge, the opening of the East River tunnels in 1910 connected the trains of Long Island to Manhattan, opening up a major new commuter network. This network was further extended in fits and starts, from the construction of the IND Flushing Line between 1915 and 1928, to the cut-and-cover extension of the IND subway line below a newly widened Queens Boulevard between 1936 and 1956.

Despite the increased availability of train connections, it was the automobile that provided the motive force for Queens' growth, catalyzed by the emergence of Robert Moses' bridge and expressway system linking Queens to Manhattan, The Bronx, New Jersey, and Upstate New York. Throughout the 1930s and 1940s, Moses invested public funds in massive automobile-oriented infrastructure projects in Queens, opening the Triboro and Throgs Neck bridges in 1936, the Whitestone Bridge in 1939, and the Midtown Tunnel in 1940. Meanwhile, under the New Deal and later the Interstate Highway Act, the city transformed Queens dramatically through the creation of major roads, expressways, and parkways. These included Interstate-linked projects such as the Brooklyn-Queens Expressway and the Long Island Expressway, as well as major connector roads such as Jackie Robinson and Cross-Island parkways.

By the closing of the World's Fair in 1940, Queens had grown to a population of 1.3 million spread unevenly across the borough's 117 acres, connected by a growing network of roads and highways. Over the next few decades, its rate of growth would slow appreciably, even while the absolute numbers increased from 1.5 million in 1950 to nearly two million in 1970. Many new residential developments filled in the borough's gaps in the postwar decades of the 1950s and 1960s, most connected to the rest of the city only by the automobile. Large-scale projects continued to reshape the borough as well, including Flushing-Meadows Park, LaGuardia and Idlewild (John F. Kennedy) Airports, Shea Stadium, Astoria and Ravenswood and power plants. If nothing else, Queens embodies all of the furious energies of twentieth century urban development, exhausted through the streets, blocks, light industries, shops, parks, cemeteries, stadiums, roads and highways of the expanding metropolitan landscape.

Building the Borough of Homes

With these infrastructure developments taking shape in stages through the first half of the twentieth century, the borough's highly varied stock mix exploded across the landscape in fits and starts, following the boom and bust cycles of the speculative real estate market. What that housing stock would look like was an open question in 1900, but by 1920 the Chamber of Commerce promoted Queens as "the borough of homes." Of course, this was a highly charged sobriquet, reflecting the common American notion that only privately owned single family dwellings constituted a proper home, and that everything else was just housing, apartments, or shelter. Still, it was a notion that powered the frantic pace of development in Queens. Indeed, 70% of all housing built in Queens by 1930 came in single-family form, compared to 18.5% in The Bronx, which was dominated by rental apartments.

Three factors of timing shaped the nature and form of housing in Queens: the increasing use of the private automobile, discussed above; the rise of housing reform movements; and the shift from small companies building a handful of homes at a time, to large firms that could construct dozens or even hundreds in multiple subdivisions.

In the first half of the twentieth century, the openness of Queens to development and its growing connection to Manhattan made it attractive for housing reformers interested to experiment with new living arrangements. Heavily influenced by the Garden City movement, reform-minded architects, housing experts, and real estate investors formed limited liability corporations to purchase land for planned residential development. Between 1910 and 1940, these corporations developed a range of new communities, including the garden apartments of Jackson Heights, the curvilinear landscape of Forest Hills Gardens, the courtyard houses of Sunnyside Gardens, and the tower blocks of Rochdale Village. With the passage of the 1937 Housing Act, the New York City Housing Authority completed Queensbridge Houses, the first in what would become a series of public housing complexes scattered across the borough, from Astoria and Woodside to Flushing and Rockaway.

Of course, while reformers racked up an array of experiments, these were episodic and limited compared to the rapid expansion of single-family homes across the borough. To accommodate swelling demand, much of the borough's build-out came at increasing economies of scale, as the small parcel improvement pattern of the nineteenth century gave way to larger corporations backed by pooled capital developing multiple parcels with greater rapidity. These larger building firms exploited the increasing availability of standardized products, such as dimensional lumber, precut roof trusses, interchangeable windows and doors. Catalogue houses such as those available from Sears and other firms also appeared throughout the borough.

To save money, developers delivered many of the single-family houses in the form of attached units, either as duplexes or rowhouses. "In the Woodside, Elmhurst, and Corona," the Chamber of Commerce noted in 1920, "hundreds of houses of the two family type, tenements and small cottages, suitable for the thrifty industrial workers are under construction." Further east, however, in neighborhoods such as Murray Hill, Bowne Park, and Auburndale, detached houses were the rule. Most newly constructed homes in this period adopted successive waves of architectural revival styles. In the 1910s and 1920s, this resulted in block after block of Tudor and Queen Anne confections, with their half-timbering, gothic gables, and diamond-paned windows, and gambrel-roofed Dutch colonials. This congeries of styles expanded with Federal rowhouses, Bungalows, and Cape Cods built in profusion from the 1920s through the 1960s.

After World War II, the pattern of "fast and cheap" housing persisted, as new subdivisions and in-fill areas cropped up across the borough. As the cost of land increased, developers added more and more row houses and apartment buildings to neighborhoods that had been comprised of single-family houses, especially on the eastern and southern periphery, and on hitherto open lands near airports and expressways. Many of the new developments of the 1950s and 1960s took extra measures to accommodate the automobile, now the overwhelmingly dominant mode of transportation in the borough. Large-scale apartment towers came with underground parking or attached multi-level garages. New rowhouse complexes replaced the postage-stamp yard spaces with driveways, both at-grade and sunken towards a basement garage. By the 1960s, Queens had gained what the other boroughs (apart from Staten Island) had not: an abundance of private single-family homes with driveways for private vehicles.

By the 1970s, much of Queens had been built up with a diverse mix of housing, commerce, industry, expressways, parks and cemeteries. New waves of real estate investment in the 1990s and 2000s, when not directed towards skyscraper construction in Long Island City, has tended to focus on higher-density apartment construction, even tearing down and replacing lower scale land uses where zoning allows. But the predominance of the single-family house remains a defining feature of the borough's residential landscape and urban culture.

Moving to Queens

So who lives in All The Queens Houses? The borough has been home to many major figures in American arts, letters, politics, and entertainment, including film and television personalities like Mary Pickford, Martin Scorsese, Michael Landon, and Al Roker; musicians Louis Armstrong, Dizzy Gillespie, Lena Horne, Tony Bennett, Art Garfunkel, Paul Simon, Cyndi Lauper, Chuck D, the Ramones, and Run-DMC; writers and political figures

Jacob Riis, Betty Friedan, Jack Kerouac, Geraldine Ferraro, Andrew and Mario Cuomo; visual and performing artists such as Joseph Cornell, Isamu Noguchi, and Candy Darling. And of course Queens is the go-to place for film and television producers who want to set the home life of their characters in the bland, repetitive landscapes of lower middle-class New York: think Archie Bunker, "Ugly" Betty Suarez, and George Constanza's parents. Many of them grew up or lived in modest homes very much like those found in the pages of this book.

It is this very feature of Queens—the modest home—that has been key to its rapid growth and tremendous social diversity. The borough opened up in the 1910s and 1920s just when large numbers of "cliff dwellers" were looking for an escape from the crowding and congestion of Manhattan. Many of these newcomers were middle-class WASP families eager to dissociate from the "alien" languages, customs, and religious practices of immigrant New York, and who could afford large houses in exclusive white enclaves. However, with rapid homebuilding and burgeoning neighborhoods, large numbers of the more well-to-do Italian, Greek, Polish, and Jewish families began moving into Queens, particular in the 1930s when the Great Depression made homebuilders desperate to sell to whoever could put cash on the table. While these groups scattered across the borough, they did form concentrations: Greeks in Astoria, Italians in Corona and Howard Beach, Poles in Ridgewood and Maspeth, and Jewish people in Forest Hills.

Meanwhile, racial segregation remained a powerful organizing force in the settlement of Queens throughout much of the twentieth century. Larger building firms tended to use racially restrictive covenants more often, so that as construction shifted away from small builders, nearly half of all new subdivisions built in Queens in the 1920s and 1930s contained racial covenants. If white neighborhood associations could not maintain segregation through racial covenants or FHA restrictions, they frequently resorted to outright hostility and violence. African-American and Afro-Caribbean enclaves grew throughout the twentieth century; in 1943, for example, Louis and Lucille Armstrong moved to Corona, while Malcolm X and Betty Shabazz settled in East Elmhurst in 1957. Thanks to sustained resistance from Black civil rights and fair housing movements, segregation has lessened across New York City over the last fifty years. But despite becoming the most diverse county in the United States, large pockets of Queens remain highly resistant to Black residential expansion.

Above all, it was the passage of the 1965 Immigration Reform Act that led to the greatest social transformation in the borough's history. While newcomers found their way into all parts of New York City, Queens received the lion's share. Even before the act's passage, Puerto Rican and Dominican families had begun relocating from Manhattan to Queens in the 1940s and 1950s, searching for larger homes and job opportunities. Throughout the 1960s and 1970s, immigrant families coming from mainland China and

Korea settled in Flushing, Elmhurst, and Auburndale in ever-increasing numbers. Families from India and Bangladesh, meanwhile, concentrated in Jackson Heights and Flushing, while migrants from Taiwan, Hong Kong, Vietnam, Thailand, and the Philippines revitalized waning neighborhoods such as Elmhurst and Woodside. A wave of immigrants from the Caribbean basin, especially Jamaica, Haiti, Trinidad, and Guyana, purchased homes and built lives in Jamaica, Hollis, Richmond Hill, and Ozone Park.

In the 1970s and 1980s, new diasporic trajectories brought increasing numbers of families from Colombia, Ecuador, Honduras, Peru, and Argentina. These newcomers found homes in many parts of the borough, but concentrated in Woodside, Jackson Heights, and Corona. Additionally, Bukharin Jews and other refugees from the Soviet Union established a vibrant community in the streets and shops of Rego Park, while Mexican and Mexican-American families carved out a place for themselves in Corona. Most recently in the 1990s and 2000s, yet new waves of immigration brought Lebanese, Yemeni, and Egyptian people to Astoria, Fujian and Hong Kong Chinese to Flushing, and Nepalese and Tibetans to the streets of Jackson Heights and Elmhurst. By the time of the 1990 U.S. Census, Queens had already become the most ethnically diverse county in the country, and its diversity has only increased to date.

Queens is the Future?

Remarkably, the housing stock of Queens accommodated all of the roiling social transformations of the last half century. As new people moved in, they reshaped their homes to suit their circumstances. Sometimes these changes have been positive, with investment in additions and maintenance, new exterior flourishes and statuary, and upgraded utilities. At other times, the changes reflect conditions of financial precarity, as when owners subdivide their houses into multiple units or squeeze in several families to save money. And since the borough is largely covered by property subdivision, the only way to expand is to tear down older homes and bulk up the lots with duplexes and apartment buildings. In all cases, the borough's unpretentious and highly adaptable vernacular landscape has proven attractive to families searching for a modest foundation for their social and economic mobility.

Much of what awaits you in the following pages, then, is the ordinary, everyday residential world of Queens. But Herrin-Ferri has delivered something wonderful. Out of the bland and the banal he has wrenched an astonishing tale of rhythm and variation—a story that could only unfold through the painstaking and exhaustive effort of surveying every block of the borough's sprawling neighborhoods. With a practiced eye, he not only records houses as information or data, but also shapes an emergent story about Queens as a place. From page to page, block to block, he introduces us to the hypnotic rhythms of the habitat that residents have made for themselves over time. It is a habitat characterized by variations on themes, repeated and modified forms, borrowed and adapted styles, all alternating between unique and ubiquitous, quirky and quotidian.

If we are to find beauty in the landscape of Queens, it will not be in the individual house, but in the flexibility, modularity, and adaptability of the stock. It will be in the jumble of styles, volumes, and scale; it will be in the flowing and abrading forms, from 61st Street to 61st Road to 61st Avenue to 61st Lane to 61st Place. Queens offers perhaps the widest wide range of housing types, architectural styles, block and street morphologies, and building classes in the city—from nineteenth-century townhouses and early twentieth-century garden apartments to glass box skyscrapers, gas stations, factories, train yards, housing projects, parks, playgrounds, big box chain stores, strip malls, junk yards, underpasses, and overpasses. And, of course, single-family homes. In the end, it is not just the increasing social diversity that will define New York and the nation for decades to come; nor is it just the increasing need for an ever-more flexible array of housing options at varied scales and tenure. Rather, what will define us is how we bring these two realities together, how we build and adapt our landscapes to suit an increasingly diverse society. And for that reason, Queens might very well point us towards the future.

WORKS CONSULTED

1. Ballon, Hilary and Kenneth Jackson, eds. Robert Moses and the Modern City: The Transformation of New York. New York: Wiley, 2007.

2. Chamber of Commerce of Queens Borough, New York City, 1910–1920. New York: L. I. Star Pub. Co., 1920.

3. Copquin, Claudia Gryvatz. The Neighborhoods of Queens. New Haven, CT: Yale University Press, 2007.

4. Goodfriend, Joyce. Before the Melting Pot: Society and Culture in Colonial New York, 1664–1730. Princeton, NJ: Princeton University Press, 1992.

5. Hanson, R. Scott and Martin E. Marty. City of Gods: Religious Freedom, Immigration, and Pluralism in Flushing, Queens. New York: Empire State Editions, 2016.

6. Kroessler, Jeffrey A. Building Queens: The Urbanization of New York's Largest Borough. New York: City University of New York, 1991.

7. Lieberman, Janet and Richard Lieberman. City Limits: A Social History of Queens. Dubuque, Iowa: Kendall Hunt Pub Co, 1983.

8. Logan, John. Ethnic Diversity Grows, Neighborhood Integration Lags Behind. Albany, NY: Lewis Mumford Center, SUNY, 2001.

9. McGovern, Brendan and John W. Frazier, "Evolving Ethnic Settlements in Queens." Focus on Geography 58, 1 (2015).

10. Plunz, Richard. A History of Housing in New York City. New York: Columbia University Press, 1990.

11. Ricourt, Milagros and Ruby Danta. Hispanas de Queens: Latino Panethnicity in a New York City Neighborhood. Ithaca, N.Y: Cornell University Press, 2002.

12. Strong, John. The Algonquian People of Long Island. New York: Empire State Press, 1997.

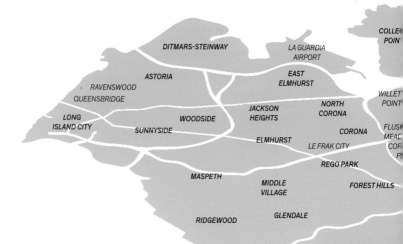

DITMARS-STEINWAY

LA GUARDIA AIRPORT

COLLEGE POINT

ASTORIA

EAST ELMHURST

RAVENSWOOD
QUEENSBRIDGE

WILLET POINT

LONG ISLAND CITY

JACKSON HEIGHTS

NORTH CORONA

WOODSIDE

SUNNYSIDE

FLUSHING MEADOWS CORONA PARK

ELMHURST

CORONA

LE FRAK CITY

REGO PARK

MASPETH

MIDDLE VILLAGE

FOREST HILLS

RIDGEWOOD

GLENDALE

WOODHAVEN

OZONE PARK

LINDENWOOD

NEW YORK CITY

HOWARD BEACH

BRONX

MANHATTAN

QUEENS

BROOKLYN

STATEN ISLAND

ROCKAWAY PARK

BELLE HARBOR

ROXBURY

NEPONSIT

BREEZY POINT

Queens Neighborhoods

Northwest
Queens

ASTORIA
DITMARS-STEINWAY
JACKSON HEIGHTS
LONG ISLAND CITY
SUNNYSIDE
WOODSIDE

Green Bay Impressions

TYPE: ROW HOUSE
BUILT: 1901 | ALTERED: 1908, 1956, 1977

These row houses are perhaps the thinnest in all of Queens at only 12.25 feet wide (3.7m) by 100 feet long (30.5m). They are also some of the oldest, dating back to 1901. As one can glean from the door pattern, there are four units in this section of the row, and each leads to a converted two-family. Like so many other early Italianates of this period, most have been wrapped in vinyl. Gone are the diamond-shaped shingles and artisanal brickwork, bracketed cornices, pedimented window frames, and projecting entry canopies. What is left, in its greatly simplified form, is a ghostly, light green impression of the traditional architecture. Even more so with this particular row since its bay window design is "pressed in" from the street wall instead of "popping out," as is typical.

French Bob Mansard
TYPE: TWO-FAMILY
BUILT: 1910 | ALTERED: C.1950, C.2010

The traditional Mansard roof style was popularized in mid-nineteenth century France, where its distinctive, dual-pitched, hipped roof profile dominated the Parisian roofscape. As it evolved from its humble garret roots into the crowning feature of most refined apartment buildings, its dormers took on an important role. The "through-the-cornice" version allowed a small portion of the façade—with a large window in it—to extend up into the roof. Fast forward one hundred years to the popular architecture culture of the United States and you have "Mansard-inspired" roof styles like the one above which omit the top roof slope, overhang the exterior wall, and extend the bulk of the façade up into the zone of the roof, evoking a "french bob" haircut.

Queens Ziggurat
TYPE: CONDOMINIUM
BUILT: 2011

Sitting on one of the most eclectic residential blocks in Queens, just south
of the Triborough Bridge on-ramp, is this unconventional mixed residential
and commercial condominium. It is one of the more striking examples of infill
housing to have been built in the borough during the last ten years. Designed
by a local Astoria firm with Greek roots, this stepped terrace structure may
evoke the old setback buildings of Manhattan to many, but given its squat
proportions and the surrounding low-to-mid-rise urban context, perhaps a
reference to antiquity is more appropriate: the ziggurats of ancient Mesopotamia.
One can only hope that in the future hanging gardens will fill its terraces.

Speckled Brick Tenement
TYPE: TENEMENT
BUILT: 1928

Before computer-generated, random pattern-making programs, there existed the art of brick blending. Bricklayers would blend in different color bricks based on percentages of brick distributed in buckets. In this tenement from the 1920s there is the ambitious attempt to do a 50/50 blend of light and dark brick. Typically, blends aren't this equal, making it easier for the bricklayer to sprinkle in bricks more evenly (see neighbor to right). This job was pretty successful until it cleared the top row of windows, where "streaks" start to appear. Nevertheless, there is a natural quality in this pattern recalling peeling tree bark or exotic fauna that contrasts sharply with the many safer computer-generated patterns so popular nowadays with designers.

Tudor Gable Bookends
TYPE: ROW HOUSE
BUILT: 1930 | ALTERED: C.1970

Most brick "colonial" row houses in Queens articulate the façade with slight setbacks, variations of brick color and patterns, or ornamental features to mark out the individual units. This long, flat, brown brick example simply uses steeply pitched gable-ends—one more than the other—with applied eaves that extend down the wall asymmetrically to connect to the corner of the original door canopy. These act as bookends for this four-unit section before the row makes a step up to adjust for the slope of the site. Their "grafted-on," autonomous quality almost seems to ignore the fenestration pattern (nicking the outside corners of the second floor windows), inadvertently producing a quasi-contemporary feel that mixes with the traditional.

Pantheon House
TYPE: CONDOMINIUM
BUILT: 1990

The Pantheon House is a typical example of post-war infill housing in Queens with the exception of its modernist façade. Normally, these small apartment buildings are clad with brown brick and feature small sliding windows with through-wall air-conditioning units located below (aka "Fedders buildings"). Here, there is a modest attempt to recreate the "heroic" characteristics of the International Style: floating white stucco volumes, ribbon windows, and cantilevered balconies fitted out with ship rails. A few red accents and six granite medallions in between the windows bring a subtle postmodern flavor into the mix—perhaps making a loose connection to the condominium's Imperial Rome building inspiration.

Minoan Makeover

TYPE: MIXED-USE
BUILT: 1901/1929 | ALTERED: 2005/2006

Behind the last stop on the N/W subway line, facing the Greek Orthodox Church of Saint Catherine and Saint George, is this simple, slightly postmodern, mixed-use, beige stucco box with five red Minoan columns. Three of them flank the entrance doors to the Cretan Association Minos Social Club at the ground level and the other two act as supports for the purely decorative cornice extensions of the upper floor addition. This one architectural detail, borrowed from the first advanced civilization of Europe, signals to the Greek community of Greater Astoria what is inside—no building sign required.

Tropical Interjection
TYPE: THREE-FAMILY
BUILT: 1945 | ALTERED: 1986

This three-family mini-tower with tropical aspirations is one of the most upbeat
architectural interjections in the borough. Apart from the bright pink monocoat—
flower pots and trash cans included!—its full-width balconies with extra doors
and windows embrace the streetscape with an open disposition. The simple
but bold decision to forgo the front door at grade makes it possible to squeeze
in the three balconies just under the building height limit, albeit not the best
idea in terms of security—for the bottom unit, at least. This is architecture
that you'd expect to see along ocean boardwalks lined with palm trees but
not in the northwest corner of Queens a block away from the East River.

We Are Happy to House You

TYPE: MULTI-FAMILY
BUILT: 1965 | ALTERED: C.1980, 2009

Even more Greek than the red Minoan columns of the previous mixed-use structure are the blue-and-white painted building features of this post-war, semi-detached, three-family walk-up. These are the predominant colors of Greater Astoria's vernacular architecture but are also a familiar combination citywide thanks to an iconic Greek-inspired coffee cup ("We Are Happy To Serve You"). Sidewalk gates, garage doors, garden pergolas, step-down awnings, eave boards, and balconies, are all tied together in a network of lightweight materials and color. As vegetation continues to grow up from the ground-level planter beds, vines will become the next prominent feature that adds life to this ordinary two-tone banded brick façade.

Tetris Stair Tower
TYPE: THREE-FAMILY
BUILT: 2004

This off-kilter tetris block of a building with uneven window heights is one of the most enigmatic residential structures in the borough. It meets the required fifteen foot setback for habitable space and yet the façade features a five-story tower-like volume with impossible floor-to-floor clearances. Upon closer inspection, these first two rows of miniature windows, plus the two rows above, and the much larger commercial size windows at the side, are all part of an elaborate, enclosed stair tower design that grants access to the three dwelling units behind while trying not to block too much light at the entry doors.

To Each Their Own (Half)
TYPE: ROW HOUSE
BUILT: 1927 | ALTERED: 1960–2020

This attached housing tract from the 1920s pairs the units in a semi-detached manner with shared roofs and a large gable front as it steps down the street in one of the hillier sections of Jackson Heights. Unlike the row in the previous spread, all the original wood-and-stucco Tudor stylings of this tract have been removed or covered up with vinyl cladding, giving it a more suburban look. The one original feature that remains is the corbelled brick chimney top. This gives the tract its curious roof profile, especially when seen from a distance. Up close, at street level, it is the front garden designs that capture one's attention. These are as varied as the population of Jackson Heights itself (the most diverse neighborhood in the borough, city, and world). In the pair of houses above, the left features a private patio with potted plants sitting atop the street wall, and at the right, a lush garden with two large trees.

To Each Their Own (Half) 2
TYPE: ROW HOUSE
BUILT: 1927 | ALTERED: 1960–2020

Just a few houses up the street is this pair of houses from the same tract. The contrast here is not as great at the garden level but higher up at the façade. This is a good example of the "harlequin phenomenon" found in much of the borough's attached (or semi-detached) housing stock: a motley combination of colors and materials coming together to define the façade of two adjacent properties. A slightly checkered quality is usually present. In this case, it is the yellow stucco base of the house on the left with the upper floor's yellow vinyl on the right. But just a few years before the above photograph was taken, this checkered quality would not have been as strong since the base of the left house was not yellow stucco, but gray granite instead. The "harlequin phenomenon" does appear regularly in Queens but given the high frequency of renovations and alterations it is just as likely to disappear as well.

Cerulean Icebox

TYPE: CONVERTED TWO-FAMILY
BUILT: 1915 | ALTERED: 1986

This house underwent a complete tonal shift when it ditched its beige-and-brown color scheme in the 80s and replaced it with an icy cerulean blue box sitting atop a faux-marble bathroom tile base. Although this bold color choice gives this building some prominence on the block, one still has to descend into a small step well to enter it. The sunken forecourt (aka, "areaway") one would expect in a situation like this, where the entry level is below grade, is missing at this house as well as its (twin) neighbor to the right, making the pair seem like they are slightly sinking into the sidewalk.

Tuscan Chapel House
TYPE: SINGLE-FAMILY
BUILT: 1920 | ALTERED: 1986

This simple yellow vinyl front with three windows, a door, and a sideways, three-step masonry stair has the spirit—and proportions—of a small Tuscan countryside chapel. It is one of the few houses in this section of Queens that has remained a single-family residence where the norm is to partition living quarters by floor and insert more windows. It did undergo an alteration in the 1980s when the roof was lifted in order to add a second story but the fenestration pattern remained unchanged, save some minor reframing, to accommodate standardized double-hung replacement units. In 1995, the same owner decided to replace a matching yellow-vinyl, single-story, cottage structure with the concrete block multi-family unit to the right.

Melting Cake Mansard
TYPE: TENEMENT
BUILT: 1931 | ALTERED: 1980

This typical wood-frame tenement fell victim to the Mansard style in the latter half of the previous century and ended up with a very bizarre top floor alteration. Some have suggested it looks like a melting cake. The addition of the faux shingle roof that notches around the third story windows produces de facto dormers that unfortunately—instead of letting light into a traditionally dark space (i.e., the attic)—block almost all sunlight that falls on this north-facing elevation. Adding to the overall strangeness of this makeover are the thin white strips posing as shutters and the half-dome canopy at the building entrance.

Fire Stair Façade
TYPE: CONVERTED MULTI-FAMILY
BUILT: 1931 | ALTERED: 1985

What looks like a back building egress stair is simply the hyper-practical solution this Queens developer employed in the 1980s to convert two tenement row houses into a multi-family residential building with increased square footage—including basement duplexes. At that time, this area of Long Island City still had a mixed-zoned character that combined residential, light industrial, and manufacturing, and perhaps this solution was not out of keeping. In today's posh Hunters Point residential landscape, this back-of-house/industrial expression is a bit shocking. Queens does have its share of exterior access stairs on mid-century buildings (and beyond) but very few with this heavy-steel type of structure that runs up the entire façade.

Gapped Tooth Triplex
TYPE: MULTI-FAMILY
BUILT: 1987

Small multi-family brick buildings with fin-wall bays are a popular typology throughout the borough. This triplex on the Sunnyside/Woodside border has an unusual gapped tooth roof profile that covers the projecting elements on the façade (bay windows and balconies). It almost has the opposite effect of the mansard-style design a couple pages back in Long Island City (*Melting Cake Mansard*), which filled the gaps between windows with unnecessary "architecture." In terms of alterations, it is not clear if the building's ironwork (railings, gates, and grilles) is trending white or black. The left unit (under different ownership), has chosen the latter while the middle and right properties prefer the more visible white color.

Sun Deli Penthouse
TYPE: MIXED-USE
BUILT: 1928 | ALTERED: 2006, 2019

Prior to the early 2000s this triangular lot along Greenpoint Avenue was just a low-slung, one-story commercial structure subdivided into two small shops. Given its difficult geometry, the property remained underdeveloped for more than eighty years until this extremely idiosyncratic two-story penthouse addition was built in 2006. Its design appears to be inspired by the architecture of warmer climates: a simple cubic volume with a flat roof, a sandy-colored stucco finish, two large patios on the second floor, a covered terrace on the third, and plenty of ventilation across its three exposures (two in the front, one in the back). A Mediterranean "villa-in-the-sky," if you will.

Happy Holdout
TYPE: TWO-FAMILY
BUILT: 1910 | ALTERED: C.1990

Sandwiched between brick warehouses, this baby blue two-family home is one of Queens' most dramatic holdouts. The block turned completely over to manufacturing in the nineties when the few remaining neighbors sold off their lots. Along with their houses went the accompanying gardens and vegetation to leave a pretty desolate streetscape with only one small street tree that is barely visible from the home's picture windows. Nevertheless, the house—and its homeowners—keep a cheerful disposition with a colorful façade and the continued use of the outdoor spaces (front terrace and rear garden).

Mint Green Duo

TYPE: CONVERTED TWO-FAMILY
BUILT: 1901 | ALTERED: C.1980, C.2010

After many renovations and alterations, these two Queen Anne houses from
the 1900s reconnected as a pair when they fell into the hands of a husband
and wife team that decided to clad them both in mint green vinyl siding and use
similar supports for their porch renovations. Unfortunately, this bond across
property lines was broken a few years after this photograph was taken when
new homeowners went their separate ways with different color schemes and
concerns with privacy. The house on the left is now painted a trendy medium
gray—base included—and has installed a new aluminum step-down awning with
an end panel blocking the view of its less renovated neighbor to the right.

Four Season Brick Frame Façade
TYPE: CONVERTED THREE-FAMILY
BUILT: 1925 | ALTERED: 2002

What began as a single-family, Folk Victorian with decorative porch detailing somehow morphed into this three-family, "four-season" sunroom extravaganza in the early 2000s. The transformation began with the conversion of the basement into a sunken two-car garage and the attic into an occupiable third level. As the design developed, the floor plates were extended into a structural steel frame that could span over the garage and accommodate a full-width sunroom at each level. This steel skeleton was then clad in brick to satisfy fireproofing standards and perhaps maintain some aesthetic continuity with the neighboring buildings.

Pixel Ghost

TYPE: CONVERTED TWO-FAMILY
BUILT: 1925 | ALTERED: C.2010

This façade that looks like an upside-down pixelated Pac-Man ghost is emblematic of the bold makeovers—albeit with questionable building materials—that occur in Queens. Twelve-inch square bathroom tile, in two tones of gray, were applied to this second story, brick-and-stone mock-Tudor to create a flat panel design with a very odd, yet somewhat iconic, character. It is not obvious what this represents, but clearly it is meant to elevate the importance of the house by amplifying the presence of the central window. In the original mock-Tudor design, this was done with rusticated stone—the reason the thin tiles stop short of the window sash on three sides.

Row House Color Blocking

TYPE: ROW HOUSE
BUILT: 1930 | ALTERED: 1933, 1953, 1986, 2020

Here is a street of row houses whose façades have been in constant flux for
the last fifty years. In the 1980s, this orange house with blind dormers that
look like fox ears used to be yellow. Its neighbor, light green. Its other neighbor,
dark green. The current (2020) color sequence is (from left to right): light
orange, pale green, beige—softer colors for sure but now combined with a
southwestern-style ashlar base on two of the houses that features even more
saturated colors than the ones in the photograph above. The original 1930s
façade concept for this row was based solely on roof and window alternation—it
actually had an interesting rhythm. But this was too subtle for Queens. Abrupt
color changes—like television color bars—are more the borough's speed.

Northeast
Queens

AUBURNDALE
BAYSIDE
BAYSIDE HILLS
BAY TERRACE
BEECHHURST
BELLEROSE
CLEARVIEW
COLLEGE POINT
DOUGLASTON
FLORAL PARK
FLUSHING
FRESH MEADOWS
GLEN OAKS
HILLCREST
HOLLIS HILLS
KEW GARDENS HILLS
LITTLE NECK
MALBA
MURRAY HILL
OAKLAND GARDENS
POMONOK
QUEENSBORO HILL
UTOPIA
WHITESTONE

Scary Tudor
TYPE: MULTI-FAMILY
BUILT: 1931 | ALTERED: C.1960

Auburndale is full of picturesque apartment buildings but this one on the corner of Crocheron Avenue and 191st Street might be the most distinctive, if not disturbing. Symmetry in the mock-Tudor style can feel menacing, especially when it produces twin shapes. And when these shapes feature tall off-kilter peaks hiding behind an extra-wide chimney decorated with crazed branch brickwork, they get even scarier. One last ingredient to highlight in this erratic mix of materials are the gray stone "errants" that have been casually "dropped" into the stucco mix of the chimney, as well as the brick base of the building. These are typical of the rustic mock-Tudor style but on this building simply add to the overall strangeness.

Ranch House in Wonderland
TYPE: SINGLE-FAMILY
BUILT: 1960 | ALTERED: 2016

This "Mediterranean" style Millennium Mansion is one of the more fantastical, if not cartoonish, alterations in the entire borough. Five years ago, it was just a half-buried, suburban Ranch house—the mirror image of the neighbor to the left (note matching garage doors). Today, it has two soaring faux brick arches (of close, but not quite equal geometry), a round stair tower with stepping windows that tuck into a corner, and more than a hundred white balusters marching across its balconies and down a long curving stair (note asymmetrical top rail pattern). In actuality, this stair is just a makeover of the original Ranch house stair with the right side of the yard excavated away to allow for two extra parking stalls. These are marked with large red diamonds, which in addition to all of the other details just described, give the new design a slightly unreal, "Alice in Wonderland" vibe.

Copacabana, Queens

TYPE: SINGLE-FAMILY
BUILT: 2005

The most striking driveway design in the borough belongs to this relatively restrained Millennial Mansion in the Northeast section of Bayside. The pattern is lifted straight from one of the most famous boardwalks in the world: the Copacabana Beach in Rio de Janeiro, designed by Brazilian landscape architect legend, Roberto Burle Marx. Unfortunately, the artisan technique of *pedras portuguesas* (small mosaic stonework) was substituted for the more economical one-foot square stone tiles. Nevertheless, this is yet another bold architectural quotation that is *bem-vindo* on the multicultural streets of Queens.

Queens Dingbat
TYPE: SINGLE-FAMILY
BUILT: 1955 | ALTERED: C.2000

Queens houses can look a bit like California ones at times. Both were developed largely in the early-to-mid-twentieth century when the automobile was a critical influence on residential design, and both employ a wide range of styles and economical materials to differentiate themselves from their neighbors. This house, with its eye-catching, flat red end elevation raised up on spindly steel columns, is like a single-family version of the "dingbat," the infamous low-rent, multi-family typology—especially popular in Los Angeles. The actual façade of this house (around the corner) is not distinctive at all: just a long, single-story ranch house profile buried into a grassy berm clad mostly in red brick.

Pumpkin Panel Floater
TYPE: SINGLE-FAMILY
BUILT: 1960 | ALTERED: C.2000

This mid-century-style Cape swapped out its original dark brown siding for pumpkin-colored metal panels at the turn of the millennium to emphasize its floating triangular roof form—a colorful, maintenance-minded, makeover that also served to differentiate it from its beige-and-brown neighbors in the same tract. Side paths provide access to the two points of entry and allow carefully trimmed hedges and trees to hide the majority of the brick base giving the house an even more weightless appearance than the previous house held up by four-inch (ten-centimeter) diameter columns.

Graves by the Bay
TYPE: TWO-FAMILY
BUILT: 1967 | ALTERED: C.2000

This small, Mansard-style, semi-detached, two-family in the car-centric neighborhood of Bay Terrace received a postmodern makeover in the early 2000s that brings to mind the vibrant colors, abstracted classical forms, and sense of humour of one of the masters of this architectural movement: Michael Graves. First, there is the "Ronald McDonald" color scheme, although the intention here was probably more "Mediterranean Villa." The next thing one notices between the two garage bay plinths is a small axis of applied ornamentation over the single central support, now reimagined as a classical fluted square column. Sitting on top of the column—instead of the expected entablature—is an empty niche shape (slightly off-center) and above this, another empty circular shape that perhaps is meant to suggest an *oeil-de-boeuf* (ox-eye window).

Red Spandrel Suburban

TYPE: TWO-FAMILY
BUILT: 1968 | ALTERED: C.2000

This slightly narrower version of the same semi-detached, two-family dwellings of the previous page trades a two-car garage for a one-car and a wider pedestrian entrance. The original, colonial-style materials—clapboard and shingles—are still intact but now feature a more graphic, red-and-white paint scheme (previously brown-and-white) that highlights the central window pattern: four double-hungs (with shutters) reading as one group and a wider set of window units with bright red clapboard spandrels that fill in the space below each window and above the garage door.

Diamonds on My Windows
TYPE: SINGLE-FAMILY
BUILT: 1925 | ALTERED: 2004

The end elevation of this single-family residence used to be just a pair of large square windows in a white stucco wall overlooking the driveway. In the early 2000s it turned into one of the most original façades in the neighborhood. The garage door opening was filled in below the belt line to create a strong base, the living room extension windows received a fanciful arched frame with diamonds, and a mostly glazed "great room" with four massive skylights crowned the whole renovation. Then a new coat of peach-colored paint was applied, with maroon accents.

Yellow Turret Two-Family

TYPE: CONVERTED TWO-FAMILY
BUILT: 1940 | ALTERED: 2004

This house is part of a full-block transformation of modest single-family Capes into converted two-family dwellings, clad mostly in brick. In almost all cases, the building envelope was expanded while maintaining some of the original openings in place, most notably the side door, which in the original house was the only door. At this corner lot, the side door has been incorporated into the new main façade, reoriented towards the side street. This provided more frontage than the original narrow façade but also produced an unbalanced composition with all the important building features located on one half of the house. The yellow bay-window towers flanking the entrance recall castle turrets.

Orange Stucco Chimney Front
TYPE: CONVERTED TWO-FAMILY
BUILT: 1936 | ALTERED: 1979, 1988, 1998, 2018

Here is another radical alteration of a single-story Cape from the 1930s into a two-story, two-family structure. The obvious remaining feature is the asymmetrical brick chimney (extended above the new roofline), which is no longer complimented by a picturesque Cape profile but instead set against a bold square of burnt orange stucco. This crosses the other conspicuous feature on the façade: a wide band of brown shingles at the top, which from the front looks like a parapet but is in fact just the build up of the new roof structure that needs to slope approximately fifty feet to the rear. Currently, the property is completely enclosed by a five foot tall vinyl fence (photograph taken on fence post installation day), which provides a buffer from this bright new front and a bit of privacy for the owner.

Greek Cross Suburban
TYPE: TWO-FAMILY
BUILT: 1983 | ALTERED: 2017

This split-level, semi-detached, two-family typology with paired garages and floating pediments can be found in many neighborhoods throughout the borough. Each has slightly different features that may include bay windows over the garage, an extra window over the front door, or faux supports for the pediment—or no supports (both appear here). In this Clearview example, the middle windows and garage doors are articulated as infill panels within a brick frame structure that reads like a Greek cross, or plus sign. It is doubtful that the architect designed this subliminal supergraphic into the façade, but regardless of their intention, once this symbol is registered on one's retina it is almost impossible to unsee.

Red Jerkinhead
TYPE: TWO-FAMILY
BUILT: 1930 | ALTERED: C.1950

The jerkinhead roof, also known as a "clipped gable," is a hybrid of the gable and hip roof forms that produces a distinctive trapezoidal gable end shape, which on this house has been clad with canary yellow vinyl siding. The rest of the façade is a red square of board-and-batten with corner trim in matching canary yellow. The offset, four-unit replacement windows speak to its two-family layout. This was even more obvious in their previous incarnation as picture windows, when the house's aesthetic leaned more mid-century suburban. Still remaining from that period are the kitschy Americana decorative touches (color-coordinated in black-and-white): vinyl shutters with flying eagle logo, panelled entry door with fanlight, and a freestanding mailbox.

Cedar Top Contemporary
TYPE: TWO-FAMILY
BUILT: 1983 | ALTERED: C.2000

This brick contemporary two-family, like the previous house, also has a hybrid roof shape consisting of a steep gable springing from a shallower hipped roof. The triangular end is infilled with cedar siding and features a large square window unit. Further complicating the roof profile is a low-pitched cross-gable at the upper unit's door serving as an entry canopy. The other highly idiosyncratic feature of this house is the exterior stair, which on the one hand appears to want to blend into the façade with its solid wall brick railing design, and on the other, reveals itself through the tread pockets that poke through the brick and a pair of openings to serve the lower level section.

Twin Gambrels
TYPE: CONVERTED TWO-FAMILY
BUILT: 2009 | ALTERED: 2020

This typology of raised two-family houses is very popular in the borough but typically features less pronounced roof profiles. Parapet walls with flat roofs are most common but there are many with shallow hipped roofs as well. This distinctive twin gambrel example manages to leverage the "attic allowance" of local zoning laws to build a third story under a "pitched roof" (fourth, if you include the garage). The hefty price to pay is for drainage. Typically, when roof shapes are paired, the most difficult water management conditions they produce are called "valleys." Here we have a ravine! Luckily, there was a little space left on the feature-filled façade (and rear elevation) to install six-foot tall scuppers with dual downspouts.

Shingle Style Color Blocking
TYPE: SINGLE-FAMILY
BUILT: 1901 | ALTERED: 2016

Among the older houses in College Point is this Shingle Style Victorian with a nicely rounded corner tower. Until recently, it was in a very dilapidated condition but a change in ownership has inspired a new wave of renovations. Apart from the brilliant azure color treatment on the bottom half that faces the corner, the house was re-clad with hexagonal shingles at the tower and clapboard at the side. Still a far cry from the "painted ladies" of San Francisco but heading in that decorative direction.

Commuter Tudor

TYPE: MULTI-FAMILY
BUILT: 1931 | ALTERED: C.1960, 2018

This apartment complex from the 1930s is a reminder of the picturesque proposition
the suburbs once offered to the Manhattan commuter. Thirty years later, this quaint
concept was overhauled and high-rise brick apartment buildings—hundreds of feet
long—would be built around the corner on the way to the commuter train station.
But residents of these Tudor apartments can still live a fantasy life from another
era within its highly articulated architectural envelope clad in a variety of traditional
materials ranging from copper to rusticated stone, all the while knowing they are
protected from evil spirits and the mortgage collector thanks to their red doors.

X-Box

TYPE: SINGLE-FAMILY
BUILT: 1950 | ALTERED: C.1980

What used to be a nondescript, boxy suburban tract house with a brick base
and a plain stucco top went for a Tudor makeover to try to differentiate itself
from its many identical neighbors. Since this was all to be surface-applied, the
traditional rustic half-timbers would have to be replaced with thin "graphic sticks."
These trace the two second floor windows to create a strong "X" pattern across
the façade and adjust the frame of the garage door to align with the picture
window on the other side of the entry door—painted red for good measure.

Triple Crown
TYPE: CONDOMINIUM
BUILT: 1996 | ALTERED: 1996–2018

The crowning feature of this multi-family walk-up is a bizarre sawtooth-like roof
profile capped with three open gables. It is only about ten feet deep giving way
to a flat roof, aligned with the low point of the open diamond shape, which covers
the rest of the structure. Originally, each unit in this building had its own recessed
balcony, providing access to fresh air. It also gave the façade more depth, and
related to the overall design, but not so much to New York, and less so Queens.
When space is limited in an urban environment—with long cold winters, no less—and
all it takes is a wall of windows to claim more for the interior, it seems to be only a
question of time before that happens. In this case, it took about twenty years.

Roosevelt Gardens

TYPE: CONDOMINIUM
BUILT: 1987

Here is another medium-sized condominium in Flushing that hints at postmodern sensibilities, this time using arches and curves to shape the front of the building. The Roosevelt Gardens experience begins curbside with an arcing path behind a full-width, crescent-shaped garden. This curving approach continues to the front door with the funnel-shaped brick walls at the ground floor of the façade. Directly above are the eyelid-shaped balconies with double-wide patio doors at the second level and a segmented arch with swing doors at the third level. Narrow corner windows and a decorative notch marking the center of the parapet provide some additional articulation that makes this even less of a big yellow brick box of a building.

Everyday Deconstructivist
TYPE: TWO-FAMILY
BUILT: 2010

This semi-detached, two-family teardown has adopted the most alien
of all architectural styles to be found in Queens: Deconstructivism. This
highly academic style that originated towards the end of postmodernism
is a little out of place in the context of the "World's Borough" due to its high
level of abstraction and total lack of sentimentality. The building's façade
employs the movement's most popular color scheme (red, white, and gray)
and then proceeds to play with our architectural expectations of symmetry,
hierarchy, and structure—most notably at the third floor balconies.

Contemporary Saltbox with Sweeping Stair
TYPE: SINGLE-FAMILY
BUILT: 1945 | ALTERED: 2008

This contemporary makeover of a typical Cape tract house strikes a modern note on this suburban street in Fresh Meadows. It is a lot more angular than the average Queens home, but its restrained material palette helps soften the edges a bit. A façade of speckled brick with the coloration of desert camouflage artfully blends with the stone-clad stair that sweeps across the front lawn to the edge of the sidewalk. The green glass fenestration feels a little commercial for this context, but the units themselves have a playful pattern that serves to animate a somewhat sombre brick wall.

Brick Block, Red Top
TYPE: THREE-FAMILY
BUILT: 1946 | ALTERED: 1998, 2015

This simple brick cube of a three-family walk-up is one of the most conspicuous structures on the suburban streets of Northeastern Queens. It sits about ten feet forward of the neighbors with a common brick front that is a story taller and capped with red masonry repair paint. Over the last thirty years, it has taken baby steps towards adopting a more residential character with renovations that include: replacing the original factory-style steel windows with white-sash sliders, replacing the wood board garage door with a white frame-and-panel version, and swapping out the flat concrete entry canopy for a gabled one with round columns. What did not help its "charm offensive" was bricking up the two existing windows over the front door and paving over the entire front yard.

Mid-century Clamshell
TYPE: SINGLE-FAMILY
BUILT: 1955 | ALTERED: C.1970

This mid-century low-rise development features Contemporary style, canted
balconies in various states of renovation and alteration. More than half are
enclosed with lightweight building materials, about a quarter in their original,
open air state, and the remainder—such as the one above—under cover, sporting
step-down awnings. Of the entire lot, this bright red one is the most conspicuous
considering its color-coordinated, clamshell appearance that contrasts sharply
with the brick-and-white "colonial" palette. This contrast is key in helping it
detach (visually) from its hidden supports (two white "toothpick" columns
and a recessed brick fin-wall) to make it "float" (architecturally speaking).

Pink Monochrome
TYPE: CONVERTED TWO-FAMILY
BUILT: 1920 | ALTERED: C. 2010

Every major American city seems to have its shockingly bright pink house. This is Queens'. It is not very accessible by foot, or from the rest of the neighborhood for that matter, and perhaps its remote location has something to do with its bold color choice: fewer neighbors, less inhibition. But that does not mean it is not seen by the rest of the borough, if not the region. Some estimated 200,000 vehicles pass by this house every day on the Long Island Expressway—located just on the other side of a service road.

Blue Curtain House
TYPE: CONVERTED TWO-FAMILY
BUILT: 1920 | ALTERED: 1956, C.2010

This is the house that faces *Pink House* on the previous page. The homeowners do not appear to be fans of their neighbor's color choice. Or perhaps they are trying to block out the expressway and exposure to those 200,000 sets of eyeballs. Either way, they have done something even more shocking and unconventional which is to install a blue curtain around their front porch. If this house was in a seaside neighborhood of The Rockaways, the attitude towards it might be very different, but in this urban setting it feels out-of-context and inappropriate—even for Queens!

French Custard Ranch House Renovation

TYPE: SINGLE-FAMILY
BUILT: 1950 | ALTERED: C.2000

This romantically inclined renovation strangely succeeded in transforming a typical mid-century suburban property into a kitschy garden pavilion fantasy. Thanks mainly to the efforts of the landscaping team, this simple hipped-roof ranch house is able to extend its "French custard" character across the whole front of the site. From the two front corners, a low scalloped wall contains the lush green lawn and topiary. Sweeping through this garden section to the right is a ceremonial stair with alternating pairs of lanterns and urns atop pedestals. For the house itself, just a few ornamental details were added: round columns flanking the garage doors that for some reason don't reach the soffit, and above, a gate-like motif made up of a baroque ironwork lintel supported by two gold-tipped posts framing the house number.

Suburban Riverboat House
TYPE: SINGLE-FAMILY
BUILT: 1955 | ALTERED: 1984 | DEMOLISHED: 2020

This is one of the most altered single-family houses in all of Queens. Nearly every aspect of the house has been modified since it was built as a one-story Tudor-style Cape: the steep roof was demolished and replaced with a fully habitable second story; rear yard additions received their own additions; a wrap-around terrace was built over those additions; and this same terrace was glazed in with a polycarbonate awning and patio door combination that makes it resembles a riverboat from the side elevation. The new color palette of red, white, and black could also be considered an alteration since the original was in the more traditional beige, brown, and brick.

Bay Window Bunker House
TYPE: SINGLE-FAMILY
BUILT: 1965 | ALTERED: C.1970

There is a slightly defensive air about this tract of semi-buried ranch homes—something almost bunker-like. For starters, they are set into a grassy embankment with carved-out driveways. Secondly, their single façade feature is a faceted bay window, designed to survey up and down the street. And finally, the ashlar stone wall behind the bay—albeit a veneer—often implies "fortification." Fortunately, there are plenty of other domestic details that belie this unfavorable impression (side decks, patio furniture, white picket stair railings, etc.) and end up producing a more ambivalent quality to the architecture.

Two-Car Suburban Saltbox
TYPE: SINGLE-FAMILY
BUILT: 1939 | ALTERED: 1958, C.2000

This single-family house altered its way out of the original colonial-inspired, split-level design of the tract to become one of the more idiosyncratic houses in this suburban section of Queens. The first alteration consisted of expanding the garage to accommodate a second car, with additional living space above daylit by a glass block corner window. An applied eave extension and wedge-shaped support fin along the right side of the triple-ganged windows subtly defines this addition as a new wing of the house. The second major alteration occurred sometime towards the end of the twentieth century/early 2000s when the whole front of the house was reclad in red brick. This gave the house a more contemporary look of compound forms blended together with one material.

Pink Brick Capriccio

TYPE: SINGLE-FAMILY
BUILT: 1945 | ALTERED: 2016

At the other end of the style spectrum (from the previous house) is this pink brick, Mediterranean-style, "capriccio." In art history terms, a *capriccio* is primarily defined as a depiction of fantastical buildings in dreamlike settings. In the context of Queens, fantastical houses, such as the one above, are frequently inserted into modest suburban streetscapes, producing an equally surreal effect. This one is packed with architectural features (portico, balcony, arcade, etc.) that give it a compressed quality—especially on the left side of the house—furthering the sensation that perhaps these are not even human proportioned spaces but just a garden folly or "pleasure pavilion" instead.

French Eclectic Cove House
TYPE: SINGLE-FAMILY
BUILT: 1925 | ALTERED: C.2000

Malba is one of the most upscale and picturesque neighborhoods of Queens with many multi-million dollar properties and views overlooking Powell's cove on the Long Island Sound. Most of the mansions are in the "Millennium" tradition: large, ostentatious, and symmetrical. This older, slightly smaller, more relaxed French Eclectic house takes its inspiration from the rambling farmhouses of France that grow in an incremental fashion, much like the majority of Queens houses, if at a reduced scale. It features a steep hipped roof over the central section and then bends and flattens to cover the asymmetrical wings of the house. The house received its yellow custard stucco finish—similar to the ranch house in Hollis Hills a few pages back—sometime in the last twenty years when the property was put up for sale. Prior to that, it was a monochrome affair with white clapboard and the same dark gray shingles.

Urban Bridge Villa
TYPE: SINGLE-FAMILY
BUILT: 1945 | ALTERED: 2001

This second house from Malba illustrates the enclave's unique urban context. Only a couple of streets, such as the one the previous house was located on, are lucky enough to be right on the Long Island Sound. The majority of them find themselves closer to the foot of the Whitestone Bridge. This house from the 1940s, with its proud, Mediterranean-style makeover, sits on one of the closer sites, with views out to the sound but also towards—and under—the bridge. From the street, its façade, and "curb appeal" is visually connected to the baby blue bridge behind it—there is even the serendipitous use of segmental arches in both structures.

Blank Façade Syndrome
TYPE: MULTI-FAMILY
BUILT: 1987

"Blank Page Syndrome" is an overwhelming sensation that plagues most students at one time or another stemming from the lack of ideas or inspiration. This could be the architectural version of that applied to residential façades. The builders even seem to be celebrating their lack of inspiration by the "blank page" of lighter color brick that fills up the façade in which four upper floor windows are set into. And yet, there is something captivating about this mostly barren façade. A quiet moment in the cluttered streetscape of Queens, an accidental Aldo Rossi design.

Spanish Revival with Chamfered Entry Tower

TYPE: SINGLE-FAMILY
BUILT: 1925 | ALTERED: C.1960

Nine blocks away from the previous residential structure is this petit Spanish Revival house, practically unchanged since it was built in 1925. Only the large fabric awnings that shaded each of the six windows on the façade have been removed—typical of most buildings of this era after the advent of air conditioning. A rare house style to find in Queens, or anywhere in the northeastern United States for that matter. Although the Spanish Revival style shares some formal similarities with its eclectic cousin, the Tudor, what distinguishes this single-family house in an interesting way—apart from the red tile roof, arched door and window tops, and heavy stucco finish—is the chamfered entry tower.

Peach Stucco Processional
TYPE: SINGLE-FAMILY
BUILT: 1945 | ALTERED: 2008

The new façade of this saltbox teardown features many elements reminiscent of Roman basilicas—or even Roman ruins—such as the open arch half supported on a single Corinthian column, and on the other side, a half-barrel, apse-like shape projecting from the plain brick. The front yard landscaping sets a nonsecular tone. A double-wide walkway of dynamic brick pavers leads straight to the front door as if it were the final stretch of a processional route, while another normal-width path crosses it and then bends towards a garden *grotto* scene complete with a Virgin Mary niche statue and a cypress tree in the background. Opposite this, standing before the "apse" of the house, is a conspicuously positioned mailbox, which in this spiritually charged context starts to look like a crucifix.

Kissing Mini-towers with Tunnel
TYPE: MULTI-FAMILY
BUILT: 2006/2014

One of the recent zoning phenomena to behold in the borough are short residential towers built halfway over the driveway easement. In most cases these remain one-sided, off-kilter constructions waiting for their neighbor to teardown and build up their "better half." The tower to the right waited eight years for its partner to arrive. This ended up being a no-frills, "Fedders building" that follows the exact same design but with a lighter brick exterior and through-wall air-conditioning units. Now the picture is complete with a "through-building" access tunnel to the rear yard parking lot.

Two-Family Belvedere
TYPE: CONVERTED TWO-FAMILY
BUILT: 1955 | ALTERED: 2005

One might expect sweeping panoramic views of the sea or countryside to legitimize a balcony addition such as this, but in Queens, extra outdoor space is always welcome and any view, even if it is towards the Long Island Expressway service road, will suffice. The initial alteration of this second floor structure was a little less classical. It consisted of skinny square posts and the ubiquitous bowed-front steel railings sitting atop the original roof. Then came the official "architectural" affirmation a few years later: faceted column covers, granite balusters, and a "Mediterranean" paint color scheme.

Yellow Ochre Federal

TYPE: CONVERTED TWO-FAMILY
BUILT: 1970 | ALTERED: 2011

Here we have one of the more striking transformations of a single-story ranch
into a quasi-traditional two-family residence. The original house featured
the popular mid-century scheme of wide-set corner windows over a two-car
garage (see previous *French Custard Ranch House* in Hollis Hills for a similar
example). The alteration swapped out these corner windows for Federal-style
ones with fanlights and then repeated the same configuration for the new
floor above. But the traditional intent of this new fenestration choice is easily
undermined by the much more modern impulse (perhaps subconscious) of
color blocking the entire façade with a smooth coat of yellow ochre stucco.

Game of Thirds
TYPE: MULTI-FAMILY
BUILT: 2006

A more playful "Fedders building" than most, this pair of three-family walk-ups is a mash-up of modern façade articulation and traditional building materials. Strip away the pre-cast balusters, bay windows, and decorative bands of yellow brick, and the simple "game of thirds" being played on its façade (two-thirds open for the top balcony, one-third open for the corner balcony below, and three-thirds open for covered entry doors at grade) would be a tenable, modern, low-rise housing design. Put all of it back, along with the frequently derided stainless steel doors, and you have a classic example of the contemporary Queens vernacular, signed and sealed by a local engineering firm, no less.

French Periscope House
TYPE: SINGLE-FAMILY
BUILT: 1947 | ALTERED: 2001

Replacing a small single-story stone-clad Cape from the 1940s, is this New Traditional French teardown, sitting on top of the old foundation. In actuality, from the eave down, this pink brick house could be of any pseudo-traditional style the borough has to offer. But from the eave up, it is unmistakably French. Set against a steep, gray shingled hipped roof (the principle identifying feature of French architectural styles) is the home's trademark: a "through-the-cornice" circular-top dormer with a full-width oculus. It is unclear from the outside what space this illuminates—most likely it is the attic, but it could be the more delightful scenario of a bathtub niche given the small window directly below that normally indicates a bathroom on the second story. Or perhaps it is not a light source at all, but a periscope to peer out over the suburban rooftops of Utopia?

Oval Pendant House

TYPE: SINGLE-FAMILY
BUILT: 1955 | ALTERED: 2006

This enigmatic façade with an oval attic window pinned to its peak like a piece of jewelry is the byproduct of a second floor makeover attempting to classicize a small mid-century home in the southern section of Whitestone. The new gable-front façade was created by introducing a (full-width) cross-gable into the original side-gabled roof so the ridges intersect at the same height. This created two valleys on either side that redirect all the rainwater to the corners of the house (note short sections of gutter). At the entrance, a new door was installed with a similar shape oval vision window, echoing the window above, while a pediment-style porch, matching the geometry of the gable, offers protection from the elements.

Brunelleschi Two-Bay
TYPE: SINGLE-FAMILY
BUILT: 1925 | ALTERED: C.1960, 1997

This single-family residence has reconnected with the spirit of its original Italianate design after going through a dark and heavy period where the porch was fully enclosed and the exterior was clad in red-and-brown asphalt shingles. The new Renaissance-inspired *loggia* at the second floor evokes the light and airy quality of the original four-bay porch, although the arches have stronger ties to Florentine *quattrocento* masters such as Filippo Brunelleschi, especially his courtyard arcade at the Basilica of San Lorenzo. But in typical Queens fashion, there is usually something amiss about the architecture: no railing at the second floor—or even access to this lofty covered space, for that matter. A *loggia* "in waiting," it would seem.

Central
Queens

CORONA
EAST ELMHURST
ELMHURST
FOREST HILLS
GLENDALE
KEW GARDENS
MASPETH
MIDDLE VILLAGE
NORTH CORONA
REGO PARK
RIDGEWOOD

Red Fedders with Solariums

TYPE: MULTI-FAMILY
BUILT: 1992 | ALTERED: C.2010, 2015

Pushed back in between two more traditional style brick-and-white trim "Fedders buildings," this twelve-unit apartment building—also a "Fedders"—features full-width solariums and a covered roof terrace. Its bright red paint scheme helps rescue what once was a dark red brick structure, with even darker horizontal bands (now painted white), from an undesirable urban recess, foregrounded by parking stalls. The bold coloring was most likely the result of embracing the patches of red masonry repair paint that began to appear on sections of the large format bricks some ten years back. Also needing an extra layer of protection at this time were the second floor solariums. This, of course, was resolved with the addition of polycarbonate awnings—the Queens panacea—layered over the curved glass eaves with almost matching profiles.

Green Elf House
TYPE: CONVERTED FOUR-FAMILY
BUILT: 1931 | ALTERED: 1974

This house, like the previous one—and many others in Queens—has also traded
in its original, more elaborated architectural features in favor of bold color. This
was a typical 1930s wood-shingled Tudor/Italianate hybrid with large divided-
lite, double-hung windows almost the size of the current front door—not the
size of the door's oval lite, as is the case now. The articulated roofline that
combines crenellations and false gables was the same but highlighted by a
band of lighter-color shingles to distinguish it from the rest of the façade. In the
current, vinyl-clad version of the house, these features now appear cartoonish
and are what gives the house a certain lighthearted/comical character.

Cutaway Fedders

TYPE: MULTI-FAMILY
BUILT: 2004

Typically, you will not see exterior stairs on multi-family buildings, but when you do they are incorporated into the design in a more architectural way. These look as if they were backside egress stairs or simply left exposed after the façade of the building magically disappeared, as in a dollhouse-style cutaway view. Adding to the effect that the façade might be "missing" are the three white pediments over the middle of each bay but with no wall underneath. Back at the ground level, the silver lining of the stair's awkward configuration is that the bottom unit resident on the right was able to fashion a garden pergola into its base—and it is bearing fruit!

Burnt Orange Makeover
TYPE: CONVERTED THREE-FAMILY
BUILT: 1925 | ALTERED: 1947, C.2010

This two-family brick house from the 1920s has been through a few alterations to arrive at this simple but bold-colored front. Unfortunately, it lost half of its windows along the way. The original façade featured ribbon windows at both floors plus a larger, matching window over the door. After going through a bizarre glass block hybrid phase that lasted until the late 2000s, the brick was stuccoed over, and this very different burnt orange-color house with a sideways stoop and a red awning was born. A conical shrub occupies the remaining ten square feet (1m^2) to the right.

East Elmhurst Gropius
TYPE: TWO-FAMILY
BUILT: 1930 | ALTERED: 2003

This two-family shares some of the graphic, "frame-and-panel" qualities of many other Queens' houses, but interprets them in the modernist fashion of the "International Style" (pioneered by German architect Walter Gropius, among others). Everything but the doghouse-style gable over the basement access door has been abstracted into a black-and-white rectilinear pattern. Perhaps even more radical than the graphic quality of the new front is the new fenestration. The windows of the original Victorian—whose cornice still peeks out from behind the extension—were evenly distributed across the façade. Here, they are consolidated at the second story as a ribbon window and replaced by a large square of glass block at the first floor—both trademarks of the modernist style.

Two Musicians

TYPE: CONVERTED THREE-FAMILY
BUILT: 1910 | ALTERED: 1976, C.2000

Perhaps no other house in Queens embodies the unintentional cubist quality found in so many semi-detached or attached properties as this converted 1900s Shingle Style residence. Originally titled "Three Musicians"—after Picasso's cubist masterpiece—this moniker was ceded to a trio of attached houses from Jamaica Hills (see p. 210) that are more reminiscent of the painting's color scheme and figure count. Yet *Two Musicians* above still remains the more cubist of the two structures. Ironically, this house owes its mismatched and fragmented quality to the fact that the property contains three units in total, not two. The left half has remained a single-family residence, while the right half refashioned itself as a two-family in the early 2000s with a new red brick façade.

Elmhurst Head House
TYPE: MIXED-USE
BUILT: 1931 | ALTERED: 1959, 1974, 1986, 1998

This is one of the more conspicuous residential structures on one of the most eclectic streets in the neighborhood of Elmhurst—just a few steps from Broadway (Elmhurst Hospital parking garage is visible beyond). Its proximity to this major thoroughfare is what increased its visibility and its ability to expand vertically thanks to the higher density zoning. Prior to this ranch house style addition on top, there was just an open terrace above the brick extension and the original gambrel roof of the Dutch colonial was fully visible from the street. At the basement level, an access canopy for the commercial portion of the property was added with a matching low-pitch gable and white vinyl siding.

Mixed-Use Buddhist

TYPE: MIXED-USE
BUILT: 2010

The everyday blend of sacred and secular is a common phenomenon in Queens.
All kinds of altars and shrines are encountered on a frequent basis walking the
streets and shopping local businesses. This architectural version combines two
floors of residential units with a Chinese Buddhist temple at grade. At first glance,
the massing of this mini-temple might be confused with the neighbor's porches,
but a second look will easily reveal the upturned, "flying eave" profile and glazed
ceramic tile characteristic of this kind of religious architecture. Underneath, on
either side of the temple's wooden doors, stone lions (*shishi*) stand guard.

Mission Glow
TYPE: TWO-FAMILY
BUILT: 1920 | ALTERED: C.2010

This minimalist, Mission-style two-family from the 1920s seems to have imported California's sunshine along with this architectural style native to the Golden State. One can sense a glow from its smooth, yellow-stucco surfaces almost a block away. Soft light filters through the polycarbonate canopy at the second-floor balcony, and a stark, de Chirico-style, set of shadows are produced by the arcaded porch below. Besides a skinny beltline above the arches, the only semblance of detail is at the subtly stepped parapet where weather stains have produced a striated pattern from the Spanish-tile coping that could almost be mistaken for an Art Deco low-relief surface treatment.

Sky Ranch

TYPE: CONVERTED TWO-FAMILY
BUILT: 1961 | ALTERED: 1990

This two-family conversion is among the most radical alterations in the borough. Its expansion over the side yard is at the second level—not first—creating a "house-in-the-sky" effect with a large covered patio below. Access to the new unit is across this patio, under the arched supports, and up a long, straight-run steel stair. Some semblance of traditional architectural balance is attempted by creating a symmetrical window composition at this new double-wide "colonial" elevation, but in the end does very little to change the dynamic nature of this addition conceived with modern materials under current zoning laws. Including the two-car garage down at street level, the property now seems fully realized as an "urban residential complex" by taking advantage of its double-wide lot and triple-level height.

Two-Family Stone Frontispiece
TYPE: TWO-FAMILY
BUILT: 1930 | ALTERED: 1951, 2002

This is one of the more peculiar two-family structures in the borough because of its degree of formality and its use of the same exact stone portico for the side elevation as it does for the main façade. In fact, the side elevation pictured above might be the more prominent of the two due to its trimmed topiary, wine-colored wood stain (front door and gable), and orientation facing a heavily trafficked avenue in the neighborhood. Also greatly helping its visibility is the height of its first floor above the sidewalk. Most houses in this historic neighborhood of Queens keep lower to the ground, but this one, in order to incorporate a one-car garage into its base, lifted its entrance almost a full floor above grade.

Tudor in Tatters

TYPE: ROW HOUSE
BUILT: 1940

This pair of attached Tudor properties a few blocks south of the historic garden district portion of the neighborhood exhibits some of the strangest and most picturesque brickwork in the borough. Originally meant to evoke the romantic charm of a dilapidated English cottage, in the rapidly urbanizing context of current Queens and the street culture of New York City at large, the façade ends up looking more like a stylish fashion garment simulating tatters. Regrettably, the neighbors to either side of this row did not continue this idiosyncratic wall treatment but stuck with the more traditional Tudor expression of half-timber frames instead.

Grafted Red Gable
TYPE: SINGLE-FAMILY
BUILT: 1940 | ALTERED: C.1970, 2019

This painted brick gable front almost looks like it was grafted onto the side of
a Cape Cod-style house—not an uncommon phenomenon across the housing
stock of this vintage in Queens, but especially strong in this example due to the
bold color scheme. The original brick-and-stucco Tudor was not high-contrast
and did not have the crisp, geometrical outlines created here with masonry
repair paint and white asbestos shingles. Instead, traditional details such as
decorative niches and tabbed masonry doors and windows—both still reading
through the thin paint job—spoke to a "storybook" attitude of episodic detailing.

Dutch Vinyl Makeover
TYPE: ROW HOUSE
BUILT: 1920 | ALTERED: 2001

A cartoonish quality has surfaced on the façade of this single-family townhouse thanks to its latest renovation. After the removal of a second floor balcony, the middle window was sealed up and a bay window was added to the porch below—a couple very common alterations in the borough, but when accompanied by a creamy vinyl cladding job with kinky green roof coping it somehow synthesizes into this peculiar, face-like image. The attic window of the Dutch gable is connected to the rest of the interior via a tapered bulkhead resembling a milk-carton on its side (slightly visible on the house to the left).

Side Elevation Crenellations
TYPE: TWO-FAMILY
BUILT: 1925 | ALTERED: 2001

The side elevation of this semi-detached two-family tract is exposed at the corner lot revealing two distinct but discordant architectural rhythms: one based on window pattern, the other, roofline. The first starts at the front of the house with a double-unit window and then alternates with two separate single-width units of the same height but unevenly spaced across the depth of the building. The second rhythm is produced by the stepping profile of the parapet crenellations that wrap around from the façade and then stretch to fill the long wall of the side elevation.

Split Gable Shingle
TYPE: TWO-FAMILY
BUILT: 1910 | ALTERED: C.1980, 2001, 2014

This 1910 Shingle-style, semi-detached house is one of the best examples
of renovated "split-face" façades in this section of Queens. Originally—in its
perfectly symmetrical state—both sides were clad with the same style shingles
and trim boards. Every architectural element and detail matched across the
property line, including a pair of oval windows in between the bay windows. In
the mid-1900s, when the two sides of the house were in need of a renovation,
new materials began to differentiate the two halves. A pale green appeared to
be the agreed-upon color. The right half used asbestos shingles, the left, vinyl
siding. Thirty years later, the contrast was made more pronounced when the left
side painted the siding beige and window trim dark red, in addition to replacing
the triple casement window of the first floor with a projecting bay unit.

Two-Family Temple
TYPE: CONVERTED TWO-FAMILY
BUILT: 1931 | ALTERED: 1971, 2008

This new residence with its narrow front and large overhangs sits on top of an old concrete block warehouse as if it were a small temple structure. To access the front door you must take a short "processional" path that starts at the almost entirely opaque property wall, through a solid peach-colored metal door, into an open-air forecourt space, and up a straight-run stair to a plinth-like terrace. From this elevated vantage point one can catch a glimpse of the "not-so-sacred" surroundings that remain in this slowly changing neighborhood: auto-repair shops and towing companies, but also the defunct Evergreen Branch of the Long Island Rail Road, which true to its name, provides a beautiful wall of trees ten feet above street level.

Mesoamerican Transformation
TYPE: CONVERTED TWO-FAMILY
BUILT: 1920 | ALTERED: 2002

This single-family residence from the 1920s featured one of the more elaborate brick façades in this central section of the borough where a large German immigrant population once lived—bricklayers included. Multiple shades of brick, architectural features (pilasters, arches, etc.), and even a patterned frieze served to decorate this stepped gable design with northern European roots. In its current stuccoed-over state, the look of the house is a lot more "Latin," reflecting recent demographic shifts in the neighborhood. Bright solid color fills the wall surfaces and the roofline recalls the profile of many Mesoamerican stepped pyramid structures.

Peach Stucco Tudor with Side Porch
TYPE: SINGLE-FAMILY
BUILT: 1920 | ALTERED: 2002

This slightly asymmetrical, front-gabled Tudor is actually a sideways, single-family structure that is part of a larger, four-unit residential complex. To the right is the left half of the semi-detached houses in the middle of the architectural composition, clad with the same traditional clay roof tile. Besides the peach-colored paint choice and the one-sided shutters at the second floor, all the original details of the house are intact—including the open side porch and the louvered attic vents. As the other houses slowly blend into the Queens vernacular with their typical alterations and additions, this one, with its distinctive color and asymmetrical façade is the one that breaks away from the pack.

Flat Arch Fedders
TYPE: MULTI-FAMILY
BUILT: 2001 | ALTERED: C.2010

Here's a "Fedders building" that got dressed up to watch the train go by. On a highly visible site a block away from the Long Island Rail Road, this triple-wide, three-family walk-up uses foam-and-stucco architectural embellishments to evoke a pseudo Renaissance Revival look. There are the flat arches of the shallow arcade that span over the sunken driveways, a segmental arched balcony frame surrounding the stacked bullnose balconies, and simpler arched door frames that just manage to squeeze in next to the mailboxes and electric meters on the ground floor. Not fully participating in the Renaissance spirit of balance and unity is the left bay property, which has fallen behind in the two-tone "Mediterranean" paint scheme.

Blue-and-White Italianate
TYPE: CONVERTED TWO-FAMILY
BUILT: 1910 | ALTERED: C.1980, 2013

One of two remaining Italianates on the block, this house is a little bit like an architectural time capsule. Although the original two-family residence from 1910 featured an open porch, two-tone hexagonal wall shingle, and a more sombre trim color (not baby blue), its tight relationship to the street and overall traditional character is a testament to the housing conventions of the past. Fast forward to contemporary Queens and a ribbon of pink and patterned brick multi-family buildings—set back a good twenty feet at either side thanks to new zoning regulations—appears to weave behind this simple blue-and-white wood frame structure putting the two eras in sharp contrast to each other.

Pink Syncopation
TYPE: CONVERTED MULTI-FAMILY
BUILT: 1935 | ALTERED: 2005

The unexpected rhythms of everyday Queens architecture are at their finest in this vertical enlargement of an existing single-story Tudor row. Balconies, bay windows, awnings, AC units, and panelled front door designs—among other less visible elements—skip from one façade to the next, sometimes in the same position, other times not; sometimes paired, other times loose; sometimes with the same design, other times a variation. In the end, all of this off-beat variety serves to blend the (almost) symmetrical trio of alterations instead of stressing their vertical property lines that are revealed by the fire parapets. The most "dynamic accent"—borrowing again from musical terminology—would have to be the recessed stairway of the middle unit, allowing a thin breach in the busy façade wall that provides some shadow and depth to the overall design.

Stepped Fedders with Applied Mansards
TYPE: MULTI-FAMILY
BUILT: 2000 | ALTERED: C.2010

This stepped "Fedders building" on a hilly street in Maspeth is of the "cliff dwelling" variety, where the expansive flat brick wall is the dominant feature, and balconies—with their associated awnings—seem to hang off of it in an independent fashion. Adding to the "vernacular" look of these specific balconies is their basket-shaped railings and misalignment across each of the three contiguous sloping properties—all clad with sandstone-color brick. Detracting from this poetic interpretation are the decorative stainless steel grilles, the matching porch awnings, and the applied mini-Mansard-style roofs. But the combination of all of these disparate elements in the design is 100% Queens.

Glass Terrace Italian-American
TYPE: CONVERTED TWO-FAMILY
BUILT: 1915 | ALTERED: 2003

This proud Italian-American alteration transformed a skinny single-story Cape into a three-story, multi-terraced, mini-tower with cruise ship-style glass balustrades. The original architects for this project were keen to replicate their design for the neighboring yellow brick buildings to the left and right. Luckily, their cookie-cutter approach was discarded and the homeowner's more personal and loftier expression won the day. His design combines a maritime attitude about massing—and railings—with traditional Italianate detailing around the doors and windows, subtly contrasting with the sage-colored stucco walls. The two flags planted at the upper deck most certainly represent the homeowner's hybrid identity but could also represent the hybrid nature of the house itself.

Renaissance Twins with Stair Chutes
TYPE: TWO-FAMILY
BUILT: 2009

These twinned, two-family teardowns exude a serious Mediterranean vibe in the middle of working-class Maspeth. Stylistically, they would probably fall under a broad Renaissance Revival classification because of the prominent double-height arches at the vertigo-inducing, chute-like stairs. A quick reminder that we are still in the cheap construction culture of Queens are the use of through-wall ("Fedders") air conditioner units and the inexplicable misalignment of the right building's windows. (Window misalignments are not a hallmark of authentic "Renaissance" architecture.) Where the architects went for a little more class was in the selection of thin profile brass metalwork—not the borough-standard of tubular stainless steel.

Mixed Masonry Two-Family

TYPE: CONVERTED TWO-FAMILY
BUILT: 1935 | ALTERED: 1936, 1939, 1944, 1967

This strange pair of Tudor-esque, stone-clad townhouses were originally very tidy wood clapboard Italianates with tall narrow windows and elegantly bracketed cornices. The first façade makeover (right-side house) was in the 1940s, followed by the left-side house in the 1960s—a loose imitation of its neighbor with different masonry colors and no gable or entry porch. Among the more unconventional, if not unsettling, aspects of these converted two-families are the roles stone and brick play on the façade. Typically, when these two materials are combined it is the brick that makes up the majority of the wall surface and the larger stones accentuate the openings (see *Commuter Tudor* from Douglaston, for example). Here it is reversed, making it appear that an irregular, cave-like opening was infilled with brick in order to accommodate a rectangular window.

Pink Stucco Princess

TYPE: CONVERTED TWO-FAMILY
BUILT: 1920 | ALTERED: 2004

A house so saccharine it would make cake frosting seem salty, this attached two-family conversion from North Corona completely disregards its gritty urban surroundings in pursuit of a fairy tale-like dream. With a smooth coat of pink stucco and decorative white architectural detailing, the contrast with its similarly proportioned neighbors is jarring on the one hand, but on the other, acts as the "glue" that bonds the houses together to form an eclectic trio in the context of the larger city block. The home's peculiar entry door configuration (one frontal, the other sideways) downplays the two-family nature of the house giving the ground floor unit prominence with a small portico and a sideways stair that shows off the balustrade. The upstairs unit gets more of a "side door" treatment located outside the main volume of the house in the 2004 horizontal extension of the original porch volume.

Bi-lateral Banner House
TYPE: CONVERTED TWO-FAMILY
BUILT: 1915 | ALTERED: 1916, C.1940, C.1980, C.2000

A few blocks away from the previous house (across Northern Boulevard) is this other eclectic "trio" anchored by the house in the center with a blended bi-lateral banner graphic (USA + Dominican Republic) and a birdcage-like balcony. It has a long history of alterations starting the year after it was built in 1916. In the 1940s, it was a basic, brick-clad building that blended with its neighbors. In the 1980s, it brightened up its appearance with a bright yellow vinyl skin job but still no balcony. In the early 2000s its colors cooled down to the current mint green and baby blue as its security detail stepped up with grilles at every wall opening and the second floor setback converted to a fully enclosed exterior space.

Yellow Bird
TYPE: CONVERTED TWO-FAMILY
BUILT: 1925 | ALTERED: C.1970, 2006

This simple Queen Anne has received the full Queens' "treatment" over the last fifty years as it evolved from a single-family suburban home to a two-family urban house just steps from the Corona Plaza subway stop. The original clapboard and shingles were swapped out for canary yellow vinyl siding during the first renovation. During the two-family conversion, a second door was added off the porch, triggering a series of alterations that would lead to the substitution of the original round wood columns for flat panel truss supports and the recreation of a semi-private outdoor space in the form of a roof deck above. Almost as conspicuous as this new informal addition with a lattice-filled railing is the kinked leg, buttress-style truss off the left side of the porch. Is it there for additional support or as an informal wing wall?

Fedders Plaza
TYPE: MIXED-USE
BUILT: 2004 | ALTERED: 2006

The "mother" of all residential awnings, this clear polycarbonate canopy covers the entire front yard of a "Fedders building" producing one of the more intriguing—if not underutilized—semi-public spaces in Queens. In other parts of the neighborhood, and borough, smaller versions of the same structure would be appropriated for informal commercial activity. In many countries around the world, one could easily find a small market of stalls filling up a space like this. Here, its only function seems to be that of protecting the lower level stairs from the elements and as overflow storage. With a loosening of the zoning laws, and a little more aesthetic consideration, it would be inspiring to see covered spaces such as these participating in the dynamic street life of the community instead of being gated off from it—as de facto "pocket plazas," if you will.

Crescent Street Temple
TYPE: SINGLE-FAMILY
BUILT: 1950 | ALTERED: 2012

At the more ostentatious end of the Queens housing spectrum is this Neoclassical millennial mansion perched up on a garage plinth like a Greek temple. Located in the highly planned "Crescents" section of the neighborhood (concentric semi-circular streets), this house is among the most acontextual in the borough (not a small category), seeing that most of its neighbors are modified Capes and raised Ranches lacking Corinthian columns and Louis XIV-style gilded gates. But all of this architectural luxury comes to an abrupt end at the roof design where a smooth stucco-finish pediment and suburban style soffit are placed directly on top of the stone columns. Classic Queens.

Smooth Baby Blue
TYPE: TENEMENT
BUILT: 1906 | ALTERED: 1972

Back when this townhouse was built it was greatly outshone by a beautiful row of ornate Italianates that populated the block. As these lost their bracketed cornices, pedimented window frames, and projecting entry canopies, their façades were reduced to the simple combination of different colored synthetic materials (asphalt shingles, brick veneer, etc.). So too became the fate of this modest Victorian, opting for a baby blue vinyl top and pink brick veneer bottom. The subtle difference here was how smoothly it absorbed the little historical detailing it had (applied shingle flares, hipped-roof entry canopy, crenellated parapet) to now become one of the more attractive fronts on the block.

Holy Zebra House
TYPE: TENEMENT
BUILT: 1930 | ALTERED: 1973

Somehow channelling the High Gothic architecture of William Butterfield, this Italianate tenement employs a banded polychromatic brick design to create one of the most bewildering and beguiling façades in the borough. Critics often derided Mr. Butterfield's style as "Holy Zebra" since many of his buildings were for religious institutions and produced a striped effect with all their pattern making. This decidedly secular structure does not seem to be at the service of any higher power but instead exists simply as a showcase of the bricklayers craftsmanship—a calling card if you will. Flemish bonds, basketweaves, and *diapering* (diamond pattern infill) are all proudly displayed. Regrettably, so is "Mr. Fedders" and a couple crudely placed sliding window units on the second floor, suddenly snapping this medieval brick tapestry fantasy back to the commonplace reality of Central Queens.

Southwest
Queens

HOWARD BEACH
OZONE PARK
RICHMOND HILL
SOUTH OZONE PARK
SOUTH RICHMOND HILL
WOODHAVEN

Pink Stucco Cape with Stone Entry Tower
TYPE: CONVERTED TWO-FAMILY
BUILT: 1930 | ALTERED: 2004

Here is one of the more unusual house-and-porch combinations in the borough. A pink-stucco, front-gabled Cape with traditional white detailing is foregrounded by a fieldstone stair and a squat, castle-like tower for an entry vestibule. No entry door is visible from the front but a tiny vertical window that adds to its defensive demeanor provides an uncanny focal point at the center of this symmetrical façade. The other windows come in pairs at the second floor and attic. Wrought iron railing work is also used to balance the composition of the façade with short sections under the right-side window and the roof of the stone vestibule "tower."

Yellow Vinyl Cape with Saltbox Porch
TYPE: SINGLE-FAMILY
BUILT: 1940 | ALTERED: 1965, 2020

This modest yellow vinyl Cape remains a single-family structure but has all the peculiar variation of a converted two-family home. The nested saltbox porch structure is especially puzzling as it appears to have a second window inserted at floor level. Perhaps it serves a space connected to the brown shed roof volume at grade but it is very difficult to say how this would be divvied up with the floor of the vestibule above. In the house's most recent renovation—two years after this photo was taken—this fenestration mystery was "solved" by removing both windows and cladding the surface with beige-colored shingles.

Broken Gable Millennial
TYPE: SINGLE-FAMILY
BUILT: 1960 | ALTERED: 2003

This postmodern teardown is one of the most formal—and symmetrical—in this
section of Queens. Its façade's "broken gable" design (broken pediment reference)
features glass block vertical strips between the tall pop-out bay windows and the
double entry door. Previously, a more car-friendly ranch-style house with a large
offset picture window and attached garage occupied the site. The new arrangement
foregoes any accommodations for the car besides the narrow drive to the left. At
the front yard, a crescent-shaped footpath connecting to the sidewalk furthers the
symmetrical design while evoking the grandeur of suburban mansion drive courts.

Suburban Rooftop Solarium
TYPE: SINGLE-FAMILY
BUILT: 1950 | ALTERED: 1969, C.2000

The previous version of this house had a more incremental, "seaside" character with a variety of window styles—including circular—cut into its white shingle clad walls and rustic stone base. After its millennial-style makeover in the early 2000s, the look became a little more sombre and a lot more suburban. The two large picture windows at the second floor were consolidated into one full-width, floor-to-ceiling, window wall unit; a similar curved-eave sunroom with a more random window pattern was replaced with a tinted glass solarium of a more even appearance; and the quirky porthole-style window next to the front door was discarded in favor of a fixed rectangular pane.

Mini-tower with Arched Brick Motif
TYPE: MULTI-FAMILY
BUILT: 1980

Multi-family, brick-clad, residential buildings are usually straight-forward affairs in Queens. They keep their building envelope simple and their window patterns regular. This tall rectangular one in Ozone Park is no different but embellishes its façade with some curious brickwork involving an arch motif. Lines of lighter brick extend from the first floor to wrap around the middle windows, creating "candy-cane" like figures and a recessed semicircular section of brick recalling eyelids. At the top of the structure, the arch theme is echoed with segmented arches cut out of the parapet walls and infilled with breezeblock. The building's entrance is accessed by a sloping paved path at the side with a stepped brick railing infilled with the same breezeblock as above.

Gray Duo
TYPE: TWO-FAMILY
BUILT: 1920/2011 | ALTERED: 1979/2015

This pair of semi-detached two-families stand side by side like a classic comic duo. They each have their own personality yet play off each other in many peculiar ways. The older one on the right has a cool gray paint finish over its stucco and stone veneer while the newer one to the left uses two tones of warm gray brick. The right one is wider with stairs oriented sideways while the left one is narrower with a frontal approach. The right one is at the property line and can only accommodate a Juliet balcony while the left one is set back and has space for a full-depth balcony. The one thing that they do match up perfectly on—besides the shared property line—are the windows. Both have white vinyl frames with divided lite inserts.

Green Stucco Makeover
TYPE: CONVERTED TWO-FAMILY
BUILT: 1930 | ALTERED: 1957, 1976

This is another atypical façade that is the result of a mixed-use conversion. In the 1950s, when the property changed to residential only, the storefront was bricked up and a mid-century picture window was inserted in its place. (Subsequently, this was changed to the current four-ganged unit seen above.) In order to homogenize the patchy brickwork and brighten up the property, a clean coat of green stucco was applied over the entirety of the façade while letting the two original stone ornaments at the top (medallion and keystone) show through as if they were pieces of jewelry. Painted green diamonds at the brick terrace and a large green trapezoid at the driveway ramp extend the scope of this colorful makeover all the way out to the curb.

Queen Anne Cartoon
TYPE: CONVERTED MULTI-FAMILY
BUILT: 1901 | ALTERED: 1983

The original Queen Anne version of this house is probably turning in its grave. One of the defining characteristics of this Victorian style is to avoid any flat wall surfaces by filling the house with architectural features and various wall textures. In San Francisco, these types of houses have been lovingly restored, thanks to the "painted ladies" movement. Here in Queens, where maintenance efforts are kept to a minimum and restoration is all but non-existent, intricate historic styles often mutate into postmodern-looking structures, like the house above. Elaborate spindlework, window trim, and wood shingles have been simplified into prefab metal supports, colored stucco, vinyl siding, and painted fieldstone patterns. The historical character of the house is lost but a new, more animated one emerges, highlighting the shapes and spaces in a more lighthearted fashion.

Queen Anne Street Blend
TYPE: CONVERTED TWO-FAMILY
BUILT: 1920 | ALTERED: 2010

This simple Queen Anne sans tower has adopted a decidedly more urban attitude in recent years. Typical of many makeovers in this section of Queens, including the previous house, a dynamic pattern is used to animate the ground level, increasing its "curb appeal" for the local market. The rest of the structure above was clad in beige vinyl that filled in one side of the bay window and the corner porch, but thankfully preserved the original shape of the arched window recess at the attic level. A subtle—but perhaps unintentional—attempt was made to blend these two very different parts of the house by using yellow brick in the *diapering* (multi-color brick) pattern. The red brick in the pattern matches the new fence color.

Samurai Helmet House
TYPE: SINGLE-FAMILY
BUILT: 1920 | ALTERED: 1979, 2012, 2018

A few minor alterations and material substitutions over the years have led to this striking tract house transformation. When it was originally built in the 1920s, it was practically indistinguishable from its brown-shingled neighbors. In the 1980s, it donned a drab gray asbestos-tile coat, while its neighbors tried on other vinyl siding colors. In the 2010s, it broke out of the pack with an attic extension that pushed out over the porch, gabled dormers at the original roof, and bright white vinyl. With the highly graphic decision to paint the eave trim black, its many roof profiles combine to evoke all types of symmetrical figures: "samurai helmet," for instance.

Watermelon Stucco Makeover
TYPE: CONVERTED TWO-FAMILY
BUILT: 1925 | ALTERED: 1950, C.2010

The homeowners of this 1920s tract house have an especially festive spirit that is evidenced by their brightly colored façade makeover and the Diwali lights dripping from the eaves. It is not the only house to have broken out of the beige-white-brown color scheme of the block-long tract (a saffron yellow house is a few doors down) but it is by far the most striking—and coordinated. Even the driveway gate plays into the arch theme that dominates this new, highly decorative, design. And the fence spikes echo the white diamond ornaments on either side of the pop-out bay on the second floor.

Green Stucco Duplex
TYPE: CONVERTED TWO-FAMILY
BUILT: 1925 | ALTERED: 2007

Two-family conversions of single-family houses are among the most common types of alterations in Queens. (This book features dozens of examples from every neighborhood.) Myriad strategies exist for accommodating a second entrance but none has attempted to do so on a sixteen-foot wide front, making this two-family the narrowest (looking) in the borough. Although the quality of construction is quite low, this green stucco façade offers a tidy package of architectural elements. Access to the two entry doors is provided by a double-wide stair that lines up with the covered balcony above. This doubles as a porch canopy and has matching stainless steel railings. On the remaining seven feet of façade are double windows, the bottom one with a fanlight to match the door transoms.

Striped Chevron House
TYPE: CONVERTED TWO-FAMILY
BUILT: 1920 | ALTERED: 2007

This Hindi-influenced home makeover begins at the gate, with the clever repurposing of sacred symbols as fence spikes. Directly above is a tubular steel armature for hanging Diwali festival lights, a holiday that is celebrated with great fanfare in this section of Queens by its large South Asian community. Other lightweight elements include the metallic balcony and porch structures, the curving steel stair, and a razor thin canopy inserted a foot below the second floor overhang. However, the main event of this makeover is the striped chevron wall pattern—one of the more accomplished examples of polychromatic brickwork in the borough.

Blue Seashells

TYPE: CONVERTED TWO-FAMILY
BUILT: 1920 | ALTERED: 1954, 2013

One way you can make your tract-house stand out is by painting it blue. But even better is to cover it with seashells beforehand. This house from the 1920s ditched its wood siding in the 1950s and found inspiration in the stucco brush with this traditional decorative pattern that adorns the entirety of its façade, including the sidewalls. As part of the two-family conversion, it also bumped out its second floor over the porch with a chamfered-corner extension that is twice the depth of its bay-windowed neighbors. Separated windows (with different curtain designs), most likely indicate a new two-bedroom room layout on the inside. In 2013, the house color improved dramatically, changing from cardboard beige to cerulean blue.

Feddersdom

TYPE: MULTI-FAMILY
BUILT: 2007

Diamond patterned buildings have a sporadic but distinguished history in architecture, starting with the Doge's Palace in Venice, later adopted by pioneers of the British Gothic Revival movement (William Butterfield, etc.), and culminating in the near-psychedelic roof tile of St. Stephen's Cathedral in Vienna (aka *Stephansdom*). This "Fedders building" from South Richmond Hill uses the same large-scale, "full-bleed" approach as the Viennese cathedral's roof (hence "Fedders*dom*") to cover its entire façade. And even though it is not a hundred feet in the air, looming over a European capital, it still makes a strong impact in the "World's Borough" sitting as it does on this humble street of South Richmond HIll.

Semi-detached with Gap

TYPE: CONVERTED TWO-FAMILY
BUILT: 1920 | ALTERED: C.1980

Of the many semi-detached house typologies that fill Queens, this tract has the curious distinction of trying to remain as detached-looking as possible. Its shallow gable porches and offset bay window towers come close but do not touch. Typically, these volumes would meld together, and paint or material changes would allow them to differentiate themselves. Most likely, it was the inherent drainage problem of paired gable-fronts that produced the deep cleavage between the two. Unfortunately, the solution is just as problematic as it creates what is jokingly referred to in the architectural profession as a "dead cat" space, which is impossible to clean.

Southeast
Queens

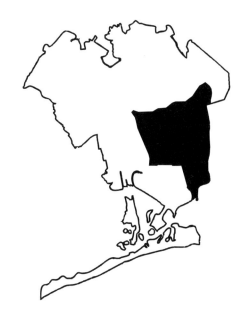

BRIARWOOD
BRICKTOWN
BROOKVILLE
CAMBRIA HEIGHTS
HOLLIS
HOLLISWOOD
JAMAICA
JAMAICA ESTATES
JAMAICA HILLS
LAURELTON
QUEENS VILLAGE
ROSEDALE
SAINT ALBANS
SOUTH JAMAICA
SPRINGFIELD GARDENS

Neapolitan Tudor
TYPE: SINGLE-FAMILY
BUILT: 1923 | ALTERED: C.1980, C.2000

The massing of this single-family Tudor has remained pretty much the same since it was built in 1923, but as the property changed hands so did the finishes. After two rounds of renovations, all the "Tudor" (i.e., half-timbers, stucco, etc.) was gone and a more modern tripartite scheme emerged looking like a vertical stack of Neapolitan ice cream (vanilla, strawberry, and chocolate). "Strawberry" must be the current homeowner's favorite since the pink stucco wraps around the other three sides of the house and down to the porch. The "vanilla" vinyl top covers what was originally the half-timbered tower expression of the house. At the base of the house and front yard, brick "chocolate" garden walls accommodate an unconventional parking stall (entered sideways) that is only accessible from the sidewalk.

Accidental Deconstructivist

TYPE: SINGLE-FAMILY
BUILT: 1928 | ALTERED: C.2000

This single-family Tudor from the 1920s went from being a subdued stucco-and-stone suburban home to a dynamic and informal one with lightweight wood and metallic extensions in every direction. At first glance, it almost looks like the original house is surrounded in scaffolding. A tall, aluminum canopy overlaps the entry porch gable with little regard for the original geometry, using triangular panels to fill in the voids; a lean-to carport connects to the left side of the house, producing an unexpected kink in the roofline; and one can only imagine what is happening at the backside of the house! In sum, a self-built assemblage with accidental deconstructivist aesthetics.

Super Dutch Shotgun
TYPE: SINGLE-FAMILY
BUILT: 1923 | ALTERED: 1984

A good decade before Super Dutch architects (Rem Koolhaas, MVRDV, etc.) started stacking suburban house shapes haphazardly, the homeowners of this shotgun house in Bricktown had a similar impulse while building their second-story addition. The shallow-gabled manufactured home we see lodged into the gable roof of the existing house overhangs the left wall a good four feet to accommodate a covered walkway to the relocated front door and side yard patio. Not likely a subversive architectural statement given the mild-mannered, beige-and-tan material palette (among other details), but still a showstopper on this quiet street of Greater Jamaica dominated by single-story pseudo-colonials.

Bluebird

TYPE: SINGLE-FAMILY
BUILT: 1960 | ALTERED: 2005

In some respects, this slightly askew, face-like façade is a logical outcome of a ranch home's vertical expansion in the context of post-millenium Queens: the two round-top "eyelid" windows plus "arched brow" dormers are centered on the upper floor; the "bird beak" bowed window below is part of the trend to replace flat, mid-century picture windows with protruding, pre-fabricated units; and bright-colored stuccoes are the finish of choice for modest makeovers such as this. The home's sky blue color ends up being the perfect choice to let these shapely white features float together like clouds in a free association puzzle.

White Castle Minimalist

TYPE: SINGLE-FAMILY
BUILT: 1994 | ALTERED 2015

What might pass for the backside of a small commercial building—loading dock and all—is actually the side elevation of one of the more abstract residential structures in the borough. The main façade of the house (facing the yard to the right) features a massive white brick wall with a narrow swath of glass block and a small front door (painted red). It is a basic minimalist design that could be found almost anywhere in the world. However, the elevation above is composed of everyday architectural elements (casement windows, balconies, garage doors) that relate to the Queens vernacular but are arranged in a more elegant manner than usual. The quirky Queens moment arrives at the parapet where two square-top, corner crenellations evoke the iconic roofline of one of the more popular fast food franchises in the borough (White Castle).

Earth-Tone Tudors
TYPE: ROW HOUSE
BUILT: 1930 | ALTERED: C.1970, C. 2010, 2016

After many years of random refinishing in a full rainbow of colors, this row is beginning to coalesce around a shared color palette of earth tones. The yellow ocre, orange pumpkin, and burgundy red paints complement each other as well as the brick highlights of the original architecture. Yet even in this moment of rare cohesion, different homeowners have different levels of appreciation for the informality of the original Tudor design. Some have chosen to highlight the erratic brick patterns, as is the case with the yellow ochre house on the left, whereas others, such as the house on the right, have color-matched the stucco to the brick in order to camouflage them.

Bluestone Frontispiece
TYPE: SINGLE-FAMILY
BUILT: 1945 | ALTERED: C.1980

This small single-family home almost appears as if it had been carved out of a suburban landscape from the past and dropped into present-day Queens. It combines two of the most popular house styles in the borough: Tudor and Cape Cod, into a tidy little asymmetrical façade foregrounded by a raised patch of lawn framed by a low-brick retaining wall. Its materials are coordinated in a cool, gray-blue palette that draw your attention straight to the Tudor-style bluestone frontispiece, with its vibrant—almost abstract art level—ashlar pattern.

Halloween in Hollis

TYPE: SINGLE-FAMILY
BUILT: 1915 | ALTERED: 2016

The northern section of Hollis is filled with large, Shingle-style Victorian homes.
These are always boxy affairs with expansive porches, clad in wood shingles, as the
name suggests. Most have replaced the original cladding with more maintenance-
friendly materials such as vinyl siding and a few have opted for stucco finishes,
at least on a portion of the house. The single-family residence above embraced
a full stucco finish and the boldest of color schemes in the neighborhood: red
and black—with matching sidewalk planter boxes. Come late October it is
probably the most popular house in Hollis—no Halloween decorations required.

Brickface

TYPE: SINGLE-FAMILY
BUILT: 1950 | ALTERED: 1970

Here is another, face-like façade—this time from the northern section of Holliswood—that represents a common figurative phenomenon in the borough. It appears on many single-family houses in the borough due to the common mid-century configuration of wide picture windows on the first floor (serving the living room or dining area) paired with two windows above (serving the bedrooms). You don't need to suffer from pareidolia (tendency to find figures or meaningful images in unintentional patterns) to spot them. But if you do, this house might also seem like it's wearing a gray flat cap and yellow gridded dress shirt.

Yellow Stucco Makeover

TYPE: TWO-FAMILY
BUILT: 1920 | ALTERED: C.1960/1999/2015/2020

This two-family residence has a long history of alterations spanning back to the 1930s when it made the bold move to widen its second floor over the recessed entries and create a completely different shape façade than that of its neighbors. The rest of the houses in the tract have more or less kept to the script: windows have been eliminated, some of the open porch corners have been closed up, but the original profile remains intact and the material changes have stayed in the conventional beige-and-brown, shingle-and-siding category. In contrast, the house above has gone "off-script" cycling through many different paint finishes and window patterns over the years trying to find a winning combination. The lemon yellow one featured here from 2019, foregrounded by a green astroturf yard and white picket fence, has been the most striking to date.

Green Supreme

TYPE: CONVERTED THREE-FAMILY
BUILT: 1935 | ALTERED: 1951

This greenest of Queens homes was always one of the most idiosyncratic since the day it was built. The uneven, slightly speckled stucco texture is actually produced from the original spotted pattern of the 1930s showing through. In addition to this folksy wall treatment, the windows had arched-top panels and the doors circular ones. Some trim boards that slightly mimicked Tudor half-timbers (still visible at the entry gable) were also part of the design. In the early 1950s, the projecting first floor volume was reconfigured with a picture window. Years later, a porch with a sunken garage was added on the side. This, of course, to be covered with a step-down awning—in green to continue the theme.

Gray Tab Two-Family

TYPE: CONVERTED TWO-FAMILY
BUILT: 1915 | ALTERED: C.1960, 1999, 2015, 2020

This quirky gray vinyl façade with a tabbed extension is the result of two very different structures slowly merging after years of alterations. Originally, there was a simple rectangular house with a flat parapet and a front-gabled garage, separated by a three foot gap. Eventually, the garage was rebuilt with a flat roof to accommodate more living space on top, including a covered terrace. A second stair was built into the gap between the structures with its access door set back a couple feet and a small canopy sticking out. The net effect of all these alterations was nothing if not chaotic. But a few years later the new puzzle-piece shaped façade (in the photo above) allowed the house to bridge the gap, incorporate the second entrance, and connect to the roofline of the covered terrace—an unplanned resolution, but one that works nevertheless.

Rose Vinyl Multi-family

TYPE: MULTI-FAMILY
BUILT: 2004

A strange creature of zoning laws and hybrid architectural styles, these contemporary townhouses are jam-packed with building features that max out the lot. Half-sunken garages provide on-site parking and reduce the overall building height to make use of the "attic allowance" for extra units under a large pitched roof. Light-and-air requirements are satisfied with covered, "flip-up" terraces and multiple skylights on each side of the gable closer to the peak. The sloping gray-shingled roof makes a reappearance over the garage doors—just a couple feet above street level—further enhancing the sunken effect of the building and its ambivalent relationship to the ground plane.

Gnome Home

TYPE: SINGLE-FAMILY
BUILT: 1940 | ALTERED: C.2010

At the other end of the Tudor spectrum (from the "Technicolor" row house vareity) is this fairy tale of a small house. Its diminutive collection of building shapes clustered around a stone patio with a winding path are a relic of Jamaica Estates' suburban past. Houses like this were meant to be "discovered" through the trees and shrubbery of suburban landscaping, similar to the placement of garden gnomes. This house cut down all of its green cover at the same time it decided to remove all of the half-timber detailing from the upper portion of the house (about five years back). It now stands fully exposed to the street at one half the size of most houses in the neighborhood—or one-quarter of the Millennial Mansion on the following page.

Opera House
TYPE: SINGLE-FAMILY
BUILT: 2005

This neo-Renaissance Millennial Mansion is next level. Of all the ostentatious mansions in Queens, none has attempted an arched portico the full width of the façade. Plenty have grand stairs, specialty shape windows, and enormous wooden doors, but they typically limit the size of the portico to the middle section of the façade. This lofty five-bay expression brings to mind the grandeur of important civic building from architectural history: Florentine Renaissance structures from the fifteenth century, or—more recently and closer to home—the Metropolitan Opera House at Lincoln Center.

Pleated Roof Fedders

TYPE: MULTI-FAMILY
BUILT: 2006 | ALTERED: C.2010

Even in high-end Jamaica Estates one cannot escape the fate of a few "Fedders buildings." Granted, these are in the opposite corner of the neighborhood from houses such as *Opera House*, but they still provide a testament to the impressive range of housing types found in one Queens zip code. Although this may not technically be considered a "Fedders building" (no through-wall air-conditioning units), it does still have all of the trappings, especially the balconies, front door cluster, and surface-mounted pipe. But its distinctive feature—every "Fedders" seems to have one—is the pleated roof design, which avoids the typical flat top that characterizes the majority of these buildings. Of course, it is not an authentic pleated roof that runs the whole depth of the building but simply a dormer-like modification of two hip roofs as they near the façade.

Blue Tudor with Glass Block
TYPE: CONVERTED TWO-FAMILY
BUILT: 1930 | ALTERED: 1943, 2020

This tract house of a different color is part of a row of mock-Tudors with alternating roof profiles, but identical interior layouts. It's hard to say which of the two is more unusual: the steep-pitched gables embedded into shed-style dormers, or the jerkinhead (clipped) dormers sprouting from the top section of gambrel roofs with cut-out terraces below. The steep-pitched gabled house above has the most striking vinyl color facing the street but it also has the least residential-looking window replacements. Glass block is usually associated with public buildings requiring privacy (medical institutions, pool facilities, etc.), but in this case it was most likely installed to reduce the presence—both visually and acoustically—of the Grand Central Parkway and its service road, which the house is adjacent to.

Three Musicians

TYPE: ROW HOUSE
BUILT: 1915 | ALTERED: 1960–2015

These three houses almost look like they stepped out of Picasso's famous "Three Musicians" painting. The white-suited flute player on the left, the brightly colored harlequin guitar player in the middle, and the singing friar with a black robe—red in this case—on the right. Each house in the trio carries its own "instrument" (porch) and strikes a colorful note in this eclectic street performance just a block away from the busy commercial thoroughfare of Hillside Avenue in Jamaica Hills. At the left, a full-width porch alteration with bay window above; in the middle, a golden-tiled porch "pavilion" with yellow trim; at the right, a red-tiled temple-like structure on white columns with matching arched windows and applied roof structure above. Running behind all of these animated architectural features is the brick bonding and shapely parapets of the original row.

Spanish Pair
TYPE: TWO-FAMILY
BUILT: 1930 | ALTERED: 1951, C.2000

As close to California as Queens gets, this southeastern section of Laurelton contains over twenty-five blocks of highly altered Spanish Revival tract houses from the 1930s. The developers only drew from two, very similar home designs to produce the 900 plus units that make up this middle-class, Depression-Era bedroom community. Today, after decades of alterations and demographic shifts, it is hard to find two houses that are the same. The pair above are of the original design that featured a low-pitched, Spanish-tile gable and single-story entry porch. The other design featured a short tower over the entrance and a flat roof (see *Spanish Single*, p. 214). Both designs have the same projecting living room bays—now with additions built on top, for the most part—and arched wing walls with a small section of Spanish tile roof that connect to the neighbor.

Spanish Pair 2

TYPE: TWO-FAMILY
BUILT: 1925 | ALTERED: C.1970, C.2000/2015

A few blocks away from the previous house pair is this combination of sharply contrasting residential styles. Their divergent designs might have been predetermined in the early planning days of the development when the decision was made to mix and match the two house types of the tract (see previous description). The left house has broken away from all conventions with the addition of a stone-clad bar on top of the original front terrace parapet, a rough new coat of yellow stucco, and the removal of the faux buttress at the left corner. The peach-colored neighbor to the right is more in line with the majority of the makeovers preferring a more classical expression with smooth, pastel-colored stucco, white architectural detailing, and a new shallow gable roof.

Spanish Single
TYPE: CONVERTED SINGLE-FAMILY
BUILT: 1920 | ALTERED: 1951, C.1990

Here is a rare case in the Laurelton "Spanish house" tract, where neighbors broke their arched wing wall connection and put up a fence in its place. The two-part, pavilion-style "wings" that were the basis of the original design have been abandoned for a more compact, private expression on each lot. The yellow-and-brown house above does this with a two-tone, two-texture vinyl cladding which highlights the projecting living room bay. In an everyday moment of "architectural collage," the faux buttress on its left corner is clad in the contrasting yellow vinyl siding color.

Spanish Single 2

TYPE: CONVERTED SINGLE-FAMILY
BUILT: 1940 | ALTERED: C.1950, C.2000

Here is another single-family house from the same tract that has been severed from its neighbor but still keeps its side of the arched wing wall intact, like an outstretched hand. (Originally, the neighbor to the left had a triple wide arch, spanning over the driveway.) The rest of the house has undergone a folksy makeover at the base and a more typical Queens transformation on top, complete with its step-down aluminum awning. Contrary to the boxy vinyl cladding of the previous house, the graphic nature of this painted fieldstone pattern on the ground floor paired with the co-planar roof profiles of the floor above has a flattening effect that seems to hide the three-dimensional character of the original Spanish Revival design.

Tudor Row House Montage

TYPE: ROW HOUSE
BUILT: 1935 | ALTERED: C.1950, C.1990, 2013

At the other end of Laurelton are several blocks of row houses that have evolved in equally unconventional ways as their semi-detached Spanish Revival cousins in the southern section of the neighborhood. These street elevations are like a montage of architectural film strips showcasing every type of wall pattern, building feature, and ornamental motif associated with the Tudor style. The above photograph represents just a snippet of this. Black-and-white half-timbers, white-and-red gable ends, decorative brickwork, stucco panels, oriel windows, and the list goes on … Like a good movie edit, there are striking scene changes and the effect is anything but formulaic. With the influx of a large African-American and Caribbean population in the 1970s, this already great film got even better with splashes of unpredictable color as highlighted in the example above.

Tudor Row House Montage 2
TYPE: ROW HOUSE
BUILT: 1930 | ALTERED: C.2000

One of the few exceptions to the colorful renovations of Laurelton Tudors, as seen in the previous photograph and the following spread, can be witnessed in the stretch of row housing above. With the exception of the wrought iron French balcony at the far left window and an entry awning that is camouflaged with the stone cladding, all the details have been preserved with their original materials and coloring intact, including one of the most distinct half-timber patterns in the entire borough. The diagonal lattice pattern that fills the gable front over the paired-door entrance is unique to this house and three others forming part of this block-long 1930s development.

Detached Asymmetrical in Beige
TYPE: SINGLE-FAMILY
BUILT: 1930 | ALTERED: C.1940, C.1980

This asymmetrical single-family home with its trapezoidal plot of land is on one of
the more unusual blocks in the borough due to its back-to-back home development.
(The blue house on the following page is its pair.) What began as a Tudor of unequal
eaves and a nested entry porch went through a colonial phase in the second half
of the twentieth century with white architectural detailing, pale yellow clapboard,
and black shutters. It then reemerged in the millenium as a "Mediterranean"
style villa with beige stucco, brown trim, skinny casement windows, and a new
entry portico. Directly behind the front door, set back from the façade on a small
triangular section of wall, is one of the remaining quirky Tudor details that this
house has held onto but its rear neighbor has not: a "through-the-cornice" wall
dormer, now detailed in a matching brown window frame and keystone motif.

Detached Asymmetrical in Blue
TYPE: SINGLE-FAMILY
BUILT: 1930 | ALTERED: C.1940, C.1980, C.2010

Even though this asymmetrical single-family is the matching pair to the previous house, it has a completely different character—almost spiritual in nature. Thanks primarily to its Krishna-blue stucco color—which seems to cast an aura around it—this property is able to detach (visually) from the more mundane residential structures of the adjacent lots and exist in its own space. It also benefits from a full presence on the site with a bold hip roof addition to the garage and a bright baby blue balustrade at the sidewalk fence. Returning to the façade, a key detail that enhances the formal/ceremonial quality of this house (versus its back-yard neighbor on the previous page) is the stacked fan-lite fenestration in a diminishing 4-3-1 window pattern.

No Door Red Gable

TYPE: CONVERTED TWO-FAMILY
BUILT: 1940 | ALTERED: 2008

This brick-and-clapboard two-family has the only "no-door" façade on the block and is one of the more striking examples of this eccentric suburban subtype, especially since it also lacks a garage door at the front. Save the small address plaque mounted to the left edge of the brick base (above the electric meters), the house offers no clues as to which side the front door is on. In the half-dozen "no-door" examples we have seen prior to this, there is usually some architectural indication, whether that be a low railing wall (see *Mini-tower with Arched Brick Motif*, Ozone Park), or a few steps when there is a slope (see *Bay Window Bunker House*, Kew Garden Hills), or a slight notch-out at the front wall (see *Two-Car Suburban Saltbox*, Little Neck). Instead, this house sits somewhat enigmatically on its lot like a big red barn, foregrounded by a patch of grass.

Red Bean Tudor

TYPE: SINGLE-FAMILY
BUILT: 1920 | ALTERED: C.1960, C.2000

The unique stucco treatment of an overzealous artisan from the 1920s has led to one of the more surprising decorative stone patterns in a borough full of surprising stone patterns. Queens, as we have seen in myriad examples, is not shy about reimagining traditional architecture, especially Tudor architecture. This style typically features a small amount of picturesque stonework randomly inserted into stucco or brick, as we have seen in many prior examples. And the stones are rectangular or jagged, not bean shaped. Apparently, the current homeowner took a fancy to this detail and decided to highlight it in red. In an equally unconventional move, the iconic half-timbers of the Tudor style have been painted out white so as to blend with the stucco and highlight this festive pattern even more.

Mid-century Multi-family Polychromy
TYPE: MULTI-FAMILY
BUILT: 1960 | ALTERED: C.1990

The residential structure above is part of a highly altered mid-century tract occupying several blocks of Southern Rosedale. The original design started as a modernist/colonial mash-up of architectural styles, featuring red brick and white clapboard, picture windows with black shutters, and semi-recessed balconies with sliding patio doors and wrought iron supports. Except for the brick, the palette was restricted to black-and-white. In the 1960s, color started to appear on the sidewalls. Soon after, the recessed balcony niches. Fifty years later, we have multi-colored combinations like the one above: an accidental work of modern architectural polychromy or the phantom image of a demolished building with all of its interior finishes exposed?

Suburban Skulls

TYPE: TWO-FAMILY
BUILT: 1969 | ALTERED: C.2010

This pair of suburban duplexes takes us back to our perennial discussion on architectural pareidolia. (See *Bluebird*, *Brickface*, and *Peach Stucco Peekaboo*) Thanks to the new, rusty-orange paint applied to the right hand property's wood shakes, this semi-detached structure now reads like two frontispieces in the shape of skulls pasted on a brick wall. The upper floor windows read like eye sockets and the lower four-unit windows in the narrower, jaw portion of the shake, like teeth. Previously, when the shingles on the right matched, the façade read as two levels: a long second story of equally spaced double windows, and below the applied eave, two dropped bays centered over the garage door, each with their picture window.

Mini Mediterranean Makeover
TYPE: SINGLE-FAMILY
BUILT: 1950 | ALTERED: C.2000

This small single-family house with the same rusty-orange paint finish as the previous two-family follows the recent trend of "Mediterranean" makeovers in the borough. Up until the millenium, this modest Cape featured a white clapboard gable front sitting on a single-story brick base with the same porch roof supported by mid-century wrought iron columns. (A shadow line indicating the built-up stucco over the triangular gable front is visible above the windows.) The formality of this new stucco façade with white classical detailing extends out to the sidewalk with a brigade of new balusters and post cap finials. Even the vegetation has gotten more formal and "Mediterranean," with a pair of cypress trees now planted at either side of the entrance.

Green Shingle Split-Level
TYPE: CONVERTED TWO-FAMILY
BUILT: 1973 | ALTERED: C.2000

In the southeastern corner of Rosedale, on a small lobe of land hugging Hook Creek, is this split-level tract house typology. In most cases, this mid-century suburban style of house tends to have a private demeanor. These split-levels display a public attitude with their street-facing terraces—complete with cheerful patio furniture—and their courthouse-style entrance under a tall pediment-like feature. Due to the staggered nature of this architectural design, the supports for this feature (flat panel trusses) bear down at the terrace level instead of the stair landing, as one might expect. At the front yard area, Queens landscaping alterations are beginning to differentiate one property from another. In a rare act of reducing space for the car, the house on the left has traded its garage and off-street parking for a patch of green grass.

Black-and-White Piano House
TYPE: SINGLE-FAMILY
BUILT: 1935 | ALTERED: C.2000

This house took its colonial black-and-white theme to the extreme when the time came to install a new fence. Previously, there was a quaint little hedgerow that wrapped around the perimeter of the property, but this was too obtrusive for the new, open yard landscaping intentions at the front, and too low for the privacy concerns at the side yard.

Inspired by the old-world elegance of the original architecture and at peace with the fencing options readily available to the Queens contractor, the homeowner installed a chain link fence with clusters of black-and-white privacy slats, marking a strong visual rhythm along this stretch of sidewalk that recalls a reverse-key piano.

Big Gable Attached Tudors
TYPE: ROW HOUSE
BUILT: 1945 | ALTERED: 1945–PRESENT

Altered Tudor row houses are abundant in the eastern section of Saint Albans. So much so that two entries were needed to get a sense of the typical street elevation. The one above and on the following page are of the double-unit, gable-front designs that mark the beginning, middle, and end of each block. These two happen to be on the same block but dozens more of equal character can be found in the surrounding streets. They create a colorful patchwork of half-timber tops and painted brick bases everywhere you look. The hot pink example above is one of the most striking as it sits on a prominent corner of the neighborhood opposite a large school building. Apart from the bright color, the other striking aspect of these painted Tudors is how their paint jobs terminate abruptly at the property line. This is how you end up with half a hot pink painted brick like we see on the half round entry porch above.

Big Gable Attached Tudors 2
TYPE: ROW HOUSE
BUILT: 1945 | ALTERED: 1945–2020

As discussed in the previous caption, this double-unit, gable-fronted Tudor is situated in the middle of the same row begun by the pair in the previous photograph. Since these rows are 600 feet long, a bold architectural moment like the one above is appreciated in order to disrupt the monotony of the basic house pattern. With this pair, there is a little more symbiosis between the two halves: both have painted their original half-timbered designs with complementary colors, preserved their slate roofing shingles, installed step-down awnings over the picture windows, and done some garden work at the front yard. The burnt sienna one on the left has been the more strident of the two with a "big bucket" approach that paints everything from the half-timbers and brick base to the awning and front steps in the same color, but has installed a front door in the same bright red as the neighbor's awnings.

Faux Gambrel with Aqua Awnings
TYPE: CONVERTED TWO-FAMILY
BUILT: 1920 | ALTERED: C.2000

This cheerful façade with aqua-colored features is a throwback to the passive cooling/pre-air-conditioning days when every door and window had an awning to protect from heat gain in the summer. These were originally a darker blue but got the "paint bucket" treatment (similar to the previous house) towards the end of the last century in an attempt to brighten the house up. The signature two-stripe pattern of the step-down awnings has been covered over giving the house a more custom, unified look. The aqua color is extended to the applied eave boards which pay homage to the early Dutch influence in Queens suggesting a gambrel roof with dormers beyond, when in reality the house is just a low-pitched gable box like its neighbors, rotated ninety degrees.

Ghostface Rowhouse with Yellow Awnings
TYPE: ROW HOUSE
BUILT: 1945 | ALTERED: C.1960, C.2000

This attached house looks as if the aqua awning house to the left and the Tudor rows of the previous spread had a baby—and the awnings came out yellow. (The same large gable roof profile exists if the faceted slate shingle roofs of the corner entry pieces are factored into the equation.) It was probably not the architect's original desire that these shapes appear melded together as they do in today's modern condition, but given the shared geometry, some of this compound form was clearly predetermined on the drafting board. Another postmodernist reading one can make with this elevation is of a single-story, vinyl-clad home dropped into the brick row from above—similar in spirit to *Elmhurst Head House* (see p.122).

Tudor and the Starfish

TYPE: TWO-FAMILY
BUILT: 1935 | ALTERED: C.1980, C.2000

This pair of semi-detached houses belongs to one of the most peculiar tracts in all of Southeast Queens, straddling the Saint Albans/Hollis border but resting mostly in Saint Albans. It is composed of four short blocks that run perpendicular to the typical street pattern, and each side of the street has four matching pairs of houses. Of the four sets of houses, the pair above belongs to the rogue pattern featuring French-inflected Tudor roofs over pop-out living room bays. (The other three feature gabled porch structures and jerkinhead dormers.) The tract is well preserved except at the detail level, where the typical replacements of minor building elements—eave boards, windows, door grilles, gutters—have been made. (New awnings were added too, of course.) Since these replacements are white, the highly idiosyncratic roof profiles that look like fragments of stars read stronger than ever.

Everyday Palladian
TYPE: SINGLE-FAMILY
BUILT: 1934 | ALTERED: 1955, C.2010

This single-family Cape has undergone a series of minor alterations in the last ten years that have produced an eye-catching façade of very humble proportions. First there were the minor shifts at the front porch which grew a wing when the right pair of windows (and wall) decided to push forward a couple feet. Then the first floor was repainted burnt sienna creating a strong dichotomy between the masonry base and the roof. Thanks to the black-on-white, graphic nature of the eave boards (similar to *Samurai Helmet House* of South Ozone Park), the roof profiles of the three different volumes extending back into the lot some sixty feet flatten out into a façade that looks as if it were almost in the same plane. The trick is as old as Palladio, done here in the informal manner of Southern Queens, not the high style of Venice, Italy.

Cross-Gable with Carport
TYPE: SINGLE-FAMILY
BUILT: 1935 | ALTERED: C.1980, C.2000 | DEMOLISHED: 2020

What started out as a modest 1920s Tudor with a cross-gabled entry porch was transformed into a mid-century architectural collage over time. A new, single-story, flat roof extension at the front produced a California-style carport to the left and an off-center entrance to the right. Holding the center, on axis with the pointy cross-gable above, is a square picture window unit with standard tripartite subdivisions. (The original renovation featured a more modern, gridded design of nine subdivisions.) Reinforcing the horizontal expression of the new roof extension is the split, red-and-white finish below and the breezeblock fence at the front. Unfortunately, the fence is the only thing surviving today as the property was redeveloped last year into a two-family home with twice the floor area but half the character.

White-and-Aqua Contemporary
TYPE: SINGLE-FAMILY
BUILT: 1950 | ALTERED: C.2000

As we have seen in a few earlier examples, but none as blatant as the house above, sometimes Queens looks more like Southern California or Florida than New York. This single-family Contemporary with a beadboard panelled front is a classic example of the 1950s style. It has the low-pitched gable roof, exposed beams on slender columns, a half-open façade with a large covered entry porch area, and the aforementioned beadboard wall panel with a glass transom above. Of course, many of the borough's typical building accoutrements (wrought iron railings, precast lion and lovebird finials, multi-colored brick fences) have crept into this mid-century modern house design, but the most dominant feature for sure is the aqua color paint scheme—a favorite in this section of Queens with a large Caribbean population.

Swan Neck Single-Family

TYPE: SINGLE-FAMILY
BUILT: 1923 | ALTERED: 1994

This skinny new stucco house with a sunken garage employs the same material palette as its contemporary "Mediterranean-style" cousins in the borough but with an unconventional color scheme and highly unusual window frame profile inspired by Georgian architecture. The latter is called a "swan neck" and is among the most mannered of all broken pediments. (A similar crowning element is used on many Chippendale furniture pieces.) In this crude, Queens version the "s-curves" look more like flames than swans. Most likely it is the "fiery" color scheme of the stucco finish that makes it appear that way.

Sunken Tudor Syncopation

TYPE: ROW HOUSE
BUILT: 1945 | ALTERED: 1960–2020

These modest row houses with Tudor stylings and sunken driveways are among the
most common, and recognizable, typologies in the borough. They are concentrated
in the northwestern neighborhoods of Astoria, Woodside, and Jackson Heights,
but also exist in parts of Central Queens and this unexpected development at the
southeastern border of (mainland) Queens, just across the expressway from JFK
Airport. Most have been significantly altered but the ones here in Springfield Gardens
have been so in a particularly consistent manner, using similarly inexpensive building
materials such as stucco, prefab awnings, and breezeblock that produce many
moments of unintentional "architectural syncopation." See *Pink Syncopation* (p.141)
for a prior discussion on this. The sections above and on the following page represent
two of the most dynamic moments involving abrupt changes across porch structures.

Sunken Tudor Syncopation 2
TYPE: ROW HOUSE
BUILT: 1945 | ALTERED: 1960–2020

Across the street from the previous photograph is this unexpected pairing of row houses with complimentary colors and connecting covered porches. The one on the right is among the few that have held onto the original Tudor brick balustrade and narrow-door garage beneath. The vast majority have both changed the railing design—or made it an extension of the wall below (left blue house)—and reconfigured the garage space as part of the interior of the house, adding a second entrance, often with an accompanying window. These can sometimes turn into their own miniature façade designs, more like the one in the previous photo with the glass block—especially when they enclose the porch.

The
Rockaways

ARVERNE
BAYSWATER
BELLE HARBOR
BROAD CHANNEL
EDGEMERE
FAR ROCKAWAY
NEPONSIT
ROCKAWAY BEACH
ROCKAWAY PARK
SEASIDE
WAVE CREST

Split Finish Two-Family
TYPE: CONVERTED TWO-FAMILY
BUILT: 1920 | ALTERED: C.1960, 2007/C.1960, C.2000

As we have been able to witness in this book, the "split-finish" is a popular phenomenon among the semi-detached and attached houses of Queens. With this pair, the split extends all the way out to the fence design with two very different attitudes towards lot security. Before these houses went their separate ways with brick and stone veneers they shared a large wall of tan-colored shingles. This looked especially blank due to the "missing" fourth window of the façade that doesn't quite fit over the combined porch element. The other houses in this tract take advantage of this empty wall space by enlarging the second floor window to a double or triple-size unit, as can be seen in the pair to the right. But the pair above have not added in more window area but cladding material instead. In the case of the right side house, this makes the fieldstone pattern the dominant feature of the design.

Kinderbridge House
TYPE: SINGLE-FAMILY
BUILT: 2008

This Millennial Mansion in Bayswater belongs to a recent subdivision of six practically identical single-family homes overlooking Jamaica Bay. The vast estuary and airplanes landing at JFK can be fully taken in from the balcony structure that projects over the second floor's large arched window. This conspicuous feature is rendered in a smooth beige stucco finish evoking the classic children's wood block shape that looks like a single-arch bridge. Hopefully, the rest of the house will complement this playful element in future renovations with a few personal touches that embrace the spirit of Queens. At the front garden, with its kitschy lawn ornaments and red lumber gravel stop, there are starting to be encouraging signs.

Brick-Clad Italianate with Hydraulic Balcony

TYPE: SINGLE-FAMILY
BUILT: 1925 | ALTERED: 2009

This big brick Italianate was most likely one of the many beach boarding houses built in the Rockaways some one hundred years back. In addition to having the same massing, architectural style, and window pattern as the other surviving examples, historic tax photos show a public-style entrance with a full-width, enclosed porch at the front. In its conversion to a single-family home at the beginning of the new millenium, the porch feature was replaced with one of the more original and unusual porticos in the borough. Two slender steel columns reach up to the third floor to support a bowed-railing balcony, somewhat reminiscent of Federal style entrances, but also recalling the smooth surfaces and floating quality of a hydraulic car lift.

Green Stucco Gable with Covered Balcony
TYPE: SINGLE-FAMILY
BUILT: 1920 | ALTERED: 2008

This green-stucco single-family is one of the last houses at the southern tip
of Broad Channel island, nestled within the dockside bars and restaurants. Its
façade is embellished with a few Millennial Mediterranean details (fluted columns,
decorative window frames, a gable oculus), but the main feature is a covered
second floor balcony with a Craftsman-style, white picket railing. Unfortunately,
this space seems to be all but abandoned—just like the burgundy colored
pick-up truck in the front yard—since this house, for all practical purposes, has
flipped its orientation towards the back, facing the bay. A narrow footpath along
the right side, past the neighbor's Sam Adams beer umbrellas brings you to
the house's real entrance: a side porch off the new, expansive rear deck.

White Picket Mannerist
TYPE: SINGLE-FAMILY
BUILT: 1920 | ALTERED: 1944, C.2000

An elaborate language of white pickets and lightweight supports is what defines this Cape's façade renovation. Although the renovation is recent, the inspiration most likely came from the Folk Victorian style of the late nineteenth/early twentieth centuries—before the original house was even built! Its signature feature was the decorative trim and jig-saw cut balusters applied to full-width porches. This house uses three different flat board picket profiles: a skewed spindle for the stair rail, a classic spindle for the landing at the top, and a rounded end, tongue-depressor style for the pickets overhead. The last profile is what gives the house its asymmetrical charm, with a scalloped look that relates to the head clearance of the stair at the front and an arch at the side. Ironically, the fence of this house is not made of white pickets but beige-colored brick instead!

Peach Stucco Peekaboo
TYPE: CONVERTED TWO-FAMILY
BUILT: 1920 | ALTERED: 1960, 2013

Another in the "pareidolia series" … This two-family residence started as a simple
Dutch Revival with a front-facing gambrel roof. In the 1960s, when the house was
converted from a single-family to a two-family, a "free classic" style Queen Anne
porch was added to the front. This consisted of a delicate spindlework structure with
a pedimented extension to receive a side-approach stair. In the latest renovation
of 2012, this open porch was bricked in up to the bottom of the porch roof (note
small pediment at top of stair) and a few small windows were installed. Peeking up
behind this new, rather defensive front, in a somewhat humorous fashion is still the
original gambrel end elevation, now finished in a smooth peach-colored stucco.

Tribal Headband House

TYPE: CONVERTED MULTI-FAMILY
BUILT: 1931 | ALTERED: C.1970, 2018

The façade of this six-unit, deep-lot, brick building is crowned with a folk architecture design of Tribal Art inspiration that is quite unlike the other polychromatic brickwork of Queens. It has nothing to do with the banding or diapering that we have seen in such examples as *Holy Zebra House*, or with the "full-bleed" patterns of *Striped Chevron House* or *Feddersdom*. It does share some of the same whimsy in its window accents as *Brick Mini-tower with Arches*, but with a more decorative spirit. Four rectangular panels—half with geometric infill—occupy the "forehead" area of the façade between the second-story windows and stepped parapet roofline, evoking an architectural "headband" of sorts. Nosepiece included.

Speckled Red-and-White Tile Façade

TYPE: SINGLE-FAMILY
BUILT: 1920 | ALTERED: 1960, 2012

As we have seen in every neighborhood of the borough so far, Queens is full of color. It also has a lot of speckled patterns. We have seen them executed in brick, ashlar stone, fieldstone, and even with rounded stones (see *Red Bean Tudor*). But perhaps the most audacious version is on this single-family home in Far Rockaway, with its random red-and-white irregular tile shapes. A passage from Louise Fitzhugh's 1964 children's literature classic *Harriet the Spy* comes to mind:

> "We're going to Far Rockaway. … I want you to see how this person lives, Harriet." … The houses, set back from the sidewalk with a patch of green in front, were built of yellow brick interspersed with red. It wasn't very pretty, Harriet thought, but maybe they liked their houses this way, better than those plain red brick ones in New York.

Baby Blue Citadel
TYPE: SINGLE-FAMILY
BUILT: 2005

This three-story, stepped, side elevation is one of the more enigmatic in the borough. Not only because of its irregular shape—derived from the required setback distance of the house's triangular site—but also the amount of baby blue windowless wall that is exposed to the street. Normally, one only witnesses residential walls this opaque in the city when a neighboring building has been demolished and the walls are exposed to the street. In the case of this corner lot house that never had a neighbor, privacy from the large yeshiva across the street seems to be the priority over daylight and views towards the street. What results is a compelling urban surface that almost has castle-like connotations.

Salmon Stucco Makeover
TYPE: SINGLE-FAMILY
BUILT: 1935 | ALTERED: C.1950, 1998, 2013

This single-family house with Mediterannean-style detailing is another Rockaways example of traditional homes with large porch structures that have undergone colorful new transformations (see *Peach Stucco Peekaboo* and *Dutch Duplex Conversion*). This salmon-colored stucco renovation of a 1930s Stick-style home retains all of the original windows and simply expands on the themes as more space is claimed for the interior. At the porch, five new windows of matching width were added to fill in the space to the left of the asymmetrically located post. At the floor above, the gabled roof kinks up to receive an extra bay to the right while full-depth dormers on both sides make the attic space habitable. On a detail level, it is worth noting that the top rail at the entry stair was designed so wide that it is now serving as a potted plant shelf.

Seven Door Wonder
TYPE: CONVERTED THREE-FAMILY
BUILT: 1930 | ALTERED: 1988

This low-slung residential structure in Rockaway Beach offers one of the most uncanny façades in the borough. It is listed as a three-family dwelling but offers five doors of equal size at street level. These are in a variety of pre-fabricated designs: four are white, one is painted red, two have decorative iron grilles, two have fan-shaped vision panels—but where do they all go? Turns out the two outside ones access mechanical closets. (Note square louvers next to doors.) At the second floor—where there are two more doors of equal proportions—things are even stranger. A fulcrum-like roof peak divides a full-width balcony with quaint white picket railings.

French Stucco SRO

TYPE: SINGLE ROOM OCCUPANCY
BUILT: 1920 | ALTERED: 2007

One of the most ornately decorated façades in all of Queens happens to belong to this converted single room occupancy (SRO) in Rockaway Beach. All windows have either a full classical frame or a window head mounted slightly above the double-hung units. On the flat surfaces of the new stucco finish a full catalogue of cast ornamentation, including medallions, scrolls, and festoons, has been applied. Originally, this structure was a large dark brown Shingle Style home with white trim and a full-width porch. From the front it still maintains its residential profile, but from the sides and back it reveals its "converted" status with numerous back-of-house additions and a roof extension to accommodate its increased occupant load.

Red Beach House with Garage Terraces
TYPE: TWO-FAMILY
BUILT: 1960 | ALTERED: C.1980

Here is a more compact version of the *Green Shingle Split-Level* house from Rosedale that does not stagger its floor plates but does have the same semi-recessed garages that double as terraces for the second floor. At the ground level, these volumes slide under the second floor to help define a covered entry space for the two units with a brick wall finish. A matching brick fin-wall separates one side of the semi-detached neighbor from the other so the space is shared by two doors and not four. Above, a shallow-roofed, second story with wide windows and patio doors spans from one garage terrace to another.

Blue Beach House with Roof Deck Superstructure
TYPE: CONVERTED FOUR-FAMILY
BUILT: 1929 | ALTERED: 1944, 1958, C.1990, C.2015

This brightly colored, Colonial Revival beach house is a four-unit dwelling in its current state, with three separate entrances, that offers three different experiences on each floor. The base is decidedly rustic, if not drab, with its stone-cladding and weathered "wood pallet" balustrade. The second floor used to get all the light and views through its two wide bay windows but is now in the shade thanks to the large roof deck above. This new ocean viewing platform initially projected from the attic level without obstructing the floor below, but this proved to be too far of a cantilever for the wood frame house. A return to more "classical" roots was in order with a post-and-lintel reinforcement structure that transfers the loads down to the porch columns.

Star-Spangled Shotgun

TYPE: SINGLE-FAMILY
BUILT: 1930 | ALTERED: C.2010

The communal court bungalow was a popular typology in the early development of the Rockaways for New York's working class. They consist of modest summer houses turned ninety degrees to the street and accessed via porch-lined alleys that cut through the block. The slightly taller Shotgun-style home above slides into the back alley space between two of these complexes and is the sole residence (among the bungalows) to front the street. This has given it an opportunity to turn its humble façade into a grand display of patriotism, inviting those from the neighboring courtyards to come socialize amid the color-coordinated patio furniture set out on the sidewalk.

Post-Sandy Pair

TYPE: TWO-FAMILY
BUILT: 2017

This pair of post-Hurricane Sandy houses are the replacement for the three storm-damaged bungalows that existed previously on the property. Following new flood zone regulations, the first habitable floor is elevated almost a full level above grade over a slatted storage area that lets any future storm waters filter through. Each dwelling unit is accessed by its own steel stair. The front one features a full-width porch (unfortunately shared with two large electric meters). In addition to these very practical characteristics, the houses adopt a striking paint color—especially for a beach house—that seems to emphasize their isolated context on a block that has been slow to rebuild.

Rocket House

TYPE: TWO-FAMILY
BUILT: 2018

This skinny, light brown stucco house exploits the new zoning laws allowing floor area to be redistributed vertically over two lots previously occupied by typical Rockaway bungalows. Even though it does not toe the property line in bright, patriotic colors like *Star-Spangled Shotgun* house on the previous page, it does stand proud, and tall, at the back of the lot like a small church building, or rocket ship. What would be the "forecourt," or "launchpad," in the more fantastic of the two metaphors, is dedicated to on-site parking, but nevertheless creates a dramatic approach to this two-family structure that towers over its existing single-story neighbors.

Bluesy Two-Bay Bungalows
TYPE: SINGLE-FAMILY
BUILT: 1931 | ALTERED: C.2010

Down the block and across the street from the previous house is this smaller bungalow complex with two-bay, clipped-gable façades and a new paint job. It also has a second row of houses in the back (these face the same direction and are accessed by a lane on the right). If the previous houses in these "bungalow" contexts used new zoning laws and patriotic symbolism to make striking statements with their properties, this example relies almost exclusively on its color scheme. Only a few years back these modest residential structures were in a dilapidated state and painted a light brown color resembling cardboard. With this shift into a calming blue spectrum with white detailing and a uniform railing design, this complex now has a stronger seaside identity and a degree of variety as well.

Photograph Index

Acknowledgements

The first person I would like to thank is urban planner and explorer extraordinaire Adam Tanaka. Thanks to his enthusiastic referral some five years back, The Architectural League of New York took an interest in *All the Queens Houses* and featured it in their online publication: *Urban Omnibus*. This piece by Emily Schmidt marked the beginning of a fruitful collaboration with the League which led to a well-received exhibition a few years later that attracted the attention of publishers. Many thanks to Emily and directors Rosalie Genevro and Anne Rieselbach for all their support.

Given that much of the inspiration for *All the Queens Houses* stems from Bernd and Hilla Becher, and the legacy they left at the Düsseldorf School of Photography, it is a great honor that this first book should be published in Germany by jovis. Many thanks to the editor, Tim Vogel, for embracing the project early on and to Susanne Rösler for her expert guidance with the design and production.

I am very grateful to Joseph Heathcott for his long standing interest in the project and the wonderful essay he has contributed to the book.

Throughout the whole process, from the initial book proposal to the final proofreading, I was extremely fortunate to have friends and fans of the project provide valuable feedback along the way. Many thanks to Alexandra Lange, Ines Leong, Michelle Lee Nix, Charles Nix, Cornelis Brinkman, Ged Merino, Laura Meyers, Kristian Schneider, Steven Sears, Catherine Martinez, and Alexandra Delano. A special thanks to Alexandra Ching for her many layout studies in the early stages, and to the Queens Council on the Arts for their generous financial support towards the end.

Finally, I would like to thank my family for providing me with the artistic foundation and the emotional support to complete this all-consuming project. My mother, Amparo Ferri, raised me with a keen sensibility for architecture and all things domestic. My father, the novelist Lamar Herrin, provided excellent commentary on all the text and inspired me to introduce a subtle storyline into the book. My uncle, the painter Antonio Ferri, exposed me to fantastic worlds of the imagination and instilled a love for the *paseo* in me at a young age. My wife, Miluska Manrique, was incredibly patient with my many weekend absences, but also generous enough to provide some well-directed criticism at a couple key moments in the process. And last, but not least, I want to express my deep gratitude to my ten-year old daughter, Waira—a Queens native—who was also incredibly patient with this project and kept it in her prayers every night. *Gracias* Pepe!

Imprint

© 2021 by jovis Verlag GmbH
Photographs, texts, and maps by kind permission of Rafael Herrin-Ferri.
Essay by kind permission of Joseph Heathcott.

Cover image: *Mesoamerican Transformation, 2018.* Photograph by
Rafael Herrin-Ferri.

Design and setting: Susanne Rösler
Proofreading: Michael Thomas Taylor
Lithography: Bild1Druck
Printed in the European Union

Bibliographic information published by the Deutsche Nationalbibliothek.
The Deutsche Nationalbibliothek lists this publication in the Deutsche
Nationalbibliografie. Detailed bibliographic data are available on the
Internet at http://dnb.d-nb.de.

jovis Verlag GmbH
Lützowstraße 33
10785 Berlin

www.jovis.de

jovis books are available worldwide in select bookstores. Please contact
your nearest bookseller or visit www.jovis.de for information concerning
your local distribution.

ISBN 978-3-86859-656-4